STILL WITH US

Voices of
Sibling Suicide Loss Survivors

Edited by Lena M.Q. Heilmann

STILL WITH US by Lena M.Q. Heilmann

BDI Publishers
ISBN 978-1-946637-02-4
FIRST EDITION

Cover & Layout Design: Tudor Maier
Cover Artwork: Amy Thrasher

BDI Publishers
Atlanta, Georgia

Preface

Those of us who have lost our loved ones to suicide know that one death can shatter us and change the course of our entire lives. Our loved ones are never just a statistic or a data point; they are individuals with unique interests, talents, and emotions, with whom we shared memories, who had entire lives and memories that were cut short by pain that ended in suicide. I hope that this book can provide readers with comfort, messages of hope and compassion, and offer a community of kind people whose lives have forever been impacted by suicide.

If you, or someone you are concerned about, is in emotional despair and looking for additional resources or support in the USA, you can go to warmline.org to locate peer support, text TALK to 741741, or call the National Suicide Prevention Lifeline at 1-800-273-8255. Because each organization has its own policies and procedures, if you have questions about how these organizations provide support and/or respond to calls/texts/chats, you can ask for clarifying information at any point during your conversations.

Preface

Contents

Preface......3

Introduction......9

On Being a Sibling Suicide Loss Survivor......25

I. The First Five Years of Grief......27
Retail Therapy and the Process of Mourning *(Lena Heilmann)*......29
King Stephen *(Sarah Jolly)*......33
And Then, She Was Gone *(Elliat Graney-Saucke)*......36
My Journey in my "New Normal" Without my Little Brother *(Helio Nowell)*......43
The Cake *(Barb Kulka)*......45

II. Grieving Years Five Through Ten......47

Looking For You *(Sarah)*......49
After Five Years *(Amy Thrasher)*......53
My Soulmate Sister, Danielle *(Lena Heilmann)*......57
The Clef and the Hummingbird *(Heather Sutherland)*......63
Losing Louise *(Shelby Drager)*......67
Catching Memories *(Jen)*......69
The Gift of Photographs *(Emily Reitenbach-Molina)*......71
Stronger Than the Struggle *(Mary Costello)*......73
Out of the Darkness: Prevention and Advocacy as Healing *(Corbin J. Standley)*......74
Don't Force Grief *(Lynne)*......77

III. Beyond the First Decade......81
Living with Gusto *(Tana Nash)*......83
Johnny's Little Sister *(WyKisha Thomas-McKinney)*......76
Finding a Way through the Darkness: Becoming a Sister on a Mission *(Sally Spencer-Thomas)*......90

Didi's Legacy *(Vanessa McGann)* 101
Still a Good Life *(Michelle L. Rusk)* 105
Three Brothers, Two Suicides, One Survivor *(Dennis Gillan)* 109
Michael *(Govan Martin)* 112
Transforming Grief Over Time: The Long View *(Larry Berkowitz)* 122

IV. Closing Reflections (Lena Heilmann)........ 127

Further Reading: Books and Articles that Address Losing a Sibling to Suicide........ 130

Suicide Prevention Organizations and Lived Experience Resources........ 132

On Inclusivity and Next Steps........ 133

About the Authors........ 135

References........ 145

Thank you to Amy Thrasher for the beautiful book cover artwork, which was inspired by the authors' experiences described in the following essays.

We will remember and love you forever...

In honor of:

Brian (1964 – 2015)
Carolyn (1961 – 2013)
Carson (1969 – 2004)
Denise
Erin (1978 – 2006)
Ervin (1985 – 2012)
Danielle (1988 – 2012)
David (1988 – 2010)
Helene (1951 – 1974)
James (1962 – 2011)
Johnny (1975 – 2004)
Louise (1992 – 2011)
Martin (1984 – 2011)
Mark – Forever 21
Matthew – Forever 23
Michael (1963 – 1980)
Nadine (1962 – 2004)
Pablo (1988 – 2016)
Shannon (1974 – 2010)
Stephen
Tessa (1985 – 2017)
Thomas (1985 – 2014)
TimE. (1992 – 2013)

Introduction

by Lena Heilmann

On November 22, 2012, I lost my younger sister and only sibling Danielle to suicide. Two weeks before she died, we celebrated her twenty-fourth birthday. We were not quite four years apart in age, and adulthood had brought us closer than ever. Danielle was my soulmate sister, and I didn't just talk to her every day; I talked to her constantly throughout each day. Danielle's death nearly destroyed me. Every breath I took after her death became a concerted effort, and every day I had to make the conscious decision to get up and keep surviving. I have just passed the six-year anniversary of her death, and the shape of my grief has changed, although it is always, always with me. Grief is still in every breath I take. Every day, I live my life in honor of my sister and the love we shared.

This book, *Still With Us: Voices of Sibling Suicide Loss Survivors*, is the type of book I needed when Danielle died. In those first days and weeks and months after my sister's death, I wanted compassionate examples of how to survive losing a sibling to suicide. During the initial days after her death, I would frantically ask myself: How can I move through each moment, each devastating day, and each lonely night? Weeks later, I wondered: How can I get through months of this grief? How can I possibly ever reach a one-year anniversary of not seeing my sister? My mind was reeling from the shock of processing my loss, and my heart and soul were shattered. I felt absolutely lost and utterly alone in my pain. I did not know if I could survive the pain—and, if I tried to tell myself that I *could* survive it, I had no idea *how* to do so.

Looking back at how scared and grief-stricken I was in those first weeks and months after my loss, I want to reach backwards in time, hug my younger self, and tell this terrified Lena that she will soon meet others who, just like her, have survived this terrible, traumatic loss and who have found ways to keep on surviving. That younger Lena was not alone in this journey. I am not alone in this journey. *You* are not alone in your journey.

Over the years, I have learned that one of my greatest strengths comes from talking with other sibling survivors of suicide loss about the good, the bad, and the absolute worst when it comes to our grief. The paths other sibling suicide loss survivors take may look different from mine in notable ways, but I have found, time and time again, that sibling survivors often understand more than anyone else the general shape of my path and the conflicting emotions I continue to feel as a sibling suicide loss survivor. My grief is marked by ambivalence, and sharing these complex, knotty emotions with others helps me know that I am not alone in this process and turmoil.

Although grief is so often heartbreakingly lonely (*all those memories I shared only with my sister are now mine alone to preserve*), I know I am not alone in grieving a sibling lost to suicide. After these six years of grieving and surviving, it is my turn to reach out and help connect more sibling survivors of suicide loss to each other and to *you*. No matter where you might be in your own grieving journey, I hope that some of these essays will resonate with you and give you perhaps a sense of comfort, of the knowledge that others are walking alongside you in this journey, and that others are ahead of you, forging a path to share with you, when the time comes.

Collecting and editing the essays that comprise this collection helped me heal as I held in my heart the powerful stories others shared with me. When I read the words of sibling suicide loss survivors who are ten, twenty, or thirty years out from their grief and about the love they continue to hold in their hearts and their souls for their siblings, I am reminded that I, too, can find a way to continue forward. The survivors who share their stories in this book are writing a network of shared resilience, of grieving, of living, of strength, and of commemorating the love that we have for our siblings, which will forever connect us to them.

How this book is arranged

The sibling survivors who wrote these essays share different and similar experiences of what it means to lose a sibling to suicide. You can read this book cover-to-cover, or you can turn to a specific essay or timeframe out from the loss. At the beginning of the collection, you will find pieces about loss in its earliest years (roughly the first five years of grief): on navigating through the first months and years of suicide loss, of starting important rituals and reminders we incorporate to honor our siblings, and on keeping our siblings by our sides during important life markers. In the middle of the collection are reflections on mid-term survival (years five through ten), the changes that grief can take in this middle stage, reflections about the passage of time, and how grief changes its form. In the third section of the collection are essays on longer-term survival (beyond the first decade of grief), which powerfully show that, although grief never goes away, its shape changes over the years and decades. This powerful message evoked by all of the following essays inspired this collection's title: our siblings are *still with us*.

Wherever you are in your journey, I hope these essays can speak to you.

On siblings

In *Still With Us: Voices of Sibling Suicide Loss Survivors*, a "sibling" can encompass a wide variety of definitions. A sibling might be someone like my sister: we had the same parents and the same last name. We grew up side-by-side, shared mannerisms and humor, and, in certain angles, looked alike. "Sibling" can also encompass different meanings. A sibling can be someone with whom we share one parent, or someone who was brought into a family through a marriage or other relationship. A sibling can be a cousin we love dearly. A sibling can be a close friend who is like a sibling to us. A sibling can be anyone who fulfills a sibling role in our lives.

This collection is meant for any sibling suicide loss survivor, however you define "sibling." If you feel like you have lost a sibling to suicide, then this collection of personal essays is meant for you.

On being a *survivor* of sibling suicide loss

Why do many of us call ourselves *survivors* of suicide loss? Losing a loved one to suicide is a traumatic event, and this loss can profoundly impact us for years and decades in the future. Siblings often share a unique and intense bond. A traumatic death is especially distressing to the sibling (or siblings) left behind. Suicide loss is also a significant loss for those who were not emotionally close to their siblings; this grief may include complicated emotions of regret, anger, and guilt.

For some of us, losing a sibling means literally losing a part of ourselves and our identities. According to Michelle Rusk (formerly Linn-Gust) in her book *Do They Have Bad Days in Heaven?* (2001) about her sister's death by suicide, "A suicide survivor is any person who loses someone he or she cares about to a suicide death. We become a survivor if a loved one dies by suicide (our sibling, parents, child, spouse) or if the suicide deeply affected someone close to us (our spouse's sibling, our child's best friend)" (p. 65). Facing our grief may be one of the hardest things we ever have to do, and we can claim the identity of a "survivor" of suicide loss.

Six years into my grief, I have learned much about my own grieving and survival, but I can still feel overwhelmed when I look at the rest of my life, spread out before me, without my sister's physical, hilarious, silly presence in it. Her absence catches me off-guard and absconds with my breath. How will I survive this? As T.J. Wray, in her book *Surviving the Death of a Sibling: Living Through Grief When an Adult Sibling Dies* (2003), poignantly writes, "Losing a sibling, then, can also mean losing a part of yourself, part of that special connection to the past. How do we learn to live with the broken circle that is now our family?" (p. 6). This is a question that I still ask myself, and I am grateful that I continue to find answers and hope in my friends, family, community, and my network of sibling suicide loss survivors.

This book, *Still With Us: Voices of Sibling Suicide Loss Survivors*, uses the term "suicide loss survivor" or "survivor of suicide loss" to distinguish from another type of suicide survivor: one who has survived a suicide attempt and/or suicidal despair. Parallel to, and intersecting with, the suicide loss community is a community made up of suicide attempt survivors and those who have survived their own thoughts of suicide. Therefore, for the sake of clarity and of empowering all survivors who are all part of the interjoined suicide-affected and suicide prevention communities, many people will refer to "suicide attempt survivors" or a "survivor of a suicide attempt" to refer to those who have survived an attempt. It is not also unusual for someone to encompass multiple survivor identities, including individuals who have survived or live with thoughts of suicide, and those who love people who experience suicidal despair. No matter what kind of survivor one is, we all carry an identity that is connected to surviving trauma.

Siblings: The forgotten mourners

Many sibling suicide loss survivors have shared with me their experience that friends, family, colleagues, acquaintances, and even strangers have dismissed or misunderstood the depth of our pain as siblings. Sibling survivors often speak to the experience that the people in their lives give more attention to the parents, children, and spouses who survive the suicide deaths of their loved ones. Due to being frequently dismissed, forgotten, or overlooked, we sibling suicide loss survivors might refer to ourselves as "forgotten mourners." Magdaline Halous DeSousa's book *The Forgotten Mourners: Sibling Survivors of Suicide* (2012) uses the term "forgotten mourners" to frame her experience and journey after the loss of her brother, John. DeSousa writes, "In any situation involving the loss of a child or young life, whether or not it's by suicide, the focus tends to go to the parents. After all, a parent is never supposed to outlive their child. Everyone seems to forget about the other children, or siblings, left behind. This is where the term 'forgotten mourners' comes from" (p. 12). Being a *forgotten* mourner, or the feeling that our pain is being overlooked or dismissed, can make the grief of losing a sibling even more difficult and lonely.

Other sibling loss survivors who have written about their grief also address this idea of being a forgotten mourner. According to Wray, "The sad fact is this: When an adult loses a brother or a sister, society often fails to recognize the depth of such a loss" (p. 4). Rusk suggests that sibling survivors of suicide loss have been referred to as "forgotten mourners" due, at least in part, to the little information that exists on this specific type of loss. And, whereas there is now an increase in research into the short-term and long-term effects of suicide on sibling survivors, well-meaning individuals might still overlook a sibling loss survivor's grief.

Whether or not you felt like your grief as a sibling was dismissed, I hope that you can find comfort in the following essays that give voice to the various journeys, challenges, and successes we have as sibling loss survivors.

Survivor guilt and other experiences

For many sibling suicide loss survivors, grieving our loss might include grappling with feelings of guilt or experiences of prejudice and discrimination, which can make the grieving process even more difficult.

Guilt can come in many forms. We can feel guilt as we play memories of our siblings back, over and over again, trapped in a cycle of criticizing ourselves and falling into self-blame. Whenever I get caught up in feeling guilty about times I bickered with my sister, I remember the bigger picture, which extends far beyond my relationship with her. Her traumas that resulted in her P.T.S.D. had nothing to do with me, and I know that our sibling relationship was often one of her strengths and reasons for living. I still have to work through guilt, but this sort of re-framing helps me when the guilt starts to arise.

There are also other forms of guilt that can arise after a sibling's suicide death. Rusk speaks to guilt that can arise from relief: "Guilt might overwhelm survivors because they feel relief that the loved one is free from his or her pain" (p. 75). After a suicide death, surviving loved ones frequently obsess over the what-ifs, the whys, the if-onlys. Rusk writes, "No one will ever know what could have happened 'if only' things were different. Suicide is the ultimate could have, would have, and should have. We can't go back and do it over. People who have died by suicide were coping with much more than we could have ever changed with one statement" (p. 75). The questions that we are left asking after our loved ones die are part of our grieving process. Wray defines *survivor guilt* as a sibling's "feelings of guilt or regret at being alive while his or her brother or sister has died. Some surviving siblings believe that fate missed her mark and took the wrong sibling by mistake. Many even feel as if their dead sibling's life was somehow more worthy or more valuable than their own" (p. 138). Guilt might be a common emotion after a sibling's death, but that shared experience might not lessen our own internalization of perceived guilt and self-blame. If you are feeling caught in these emotions, additional supports, like peer support, perhaps in the form of a support group, or a provider who has expertise in grief, particularly suicide loss, might help process these complicated emotions.

Some sibling loss survivors share that they have experienced discrimination regarding their sibling's death. In some communities, mental health concerns and anything related to suicide can be seen as frightening, as a secret, or as blameful. Sometimes, discrimination and certain belief systems can result in hurtful comments, in excluding survivors from different communities, and making access to bereavement care more difficult. Rusk writes, "Many years ago, survivors who experienced a suicide were forced into silence. The stigma that suicide was embarrassing and could ruin a family's reputation ran high. This silence led to many mental and physical problems because survivors feared outwardly expressing their grief in a consistent manner of bereavement. Shame and guilt overwhelmed those left behind" (p. 56). Emotions like shame and guilt can make grief worse, especially when it further isolates the survivor and separates them from feeling connected to their community.

If you feel guilt or shame related to your sibling's death, you are not alone. In fact, *any* emotion that you feel is one that another sibling survivor of suicide loss has felt. There are no right or wrong emotions when it comes to grieving a traumatic loss. The emotions that accompany such a terrible and traumatic death can be daunting to bear on our own, so it can be helpful to seek the support of a trusted friend, a reliable family member, or a compassionate and knowledgeable mental health provider. Additionally, talking about our loss at a support group or with a peer who has lived experience (especially someone who has been through a similar loss) can be beneficial in working through all of these emotions.

Postvention

Suicide prevention organizations often use the term *postvention* to describe bereavement and peer support services that are meant to support those who have lost loved ones to suicide. *Still With Us: Voices of Sibling Suicide Loss Survivors* is intended to be a postvention resource, for it seeks to support those of us who have lost loved ones to suicide. Lived experience (a term that refers to those who have first-hand knowledge and experience of certain life experiences, including surviving traumatic experiences and events) is an important part of suicide prevention work, and hearing from loss survivors about their grief and their survival is an important part of suicide prevention work.

In addition to the personal essays in this book, I have included in the book's final pages a list of important resources and organizations that can support us in our grief. Because losing a loved one to suicide can be such a difficult and unique grieving process, having grief support specific to suicide loss is often especially helpful for a survivor. And, beyond providing support and connecting bereaved individuals, postvention can also help mitigate additional suicide deaths. Those of us who are impacted by the suicide death of someone we loved (and continue to love) dearly might also struggle with our own thoughts of suicide. Postvention resources can help prevent more deaths, by reminding us that others have survived this terrible, traumatic loss, and they have found a way forward.

Suicide in the media

As is often the case in the high-profile celebrity suicide deaths, the media runs certain stories on a 24-hour cycle, splashing sensationalist headlines across our browsers and newspapers. These news stories might contain graphic descriptions of how an individual died, which can be harmful and painful to readers who themselves might currently be struggling with thoughts of suicide. These details can also be immensely triggering to those who have lost loved ones to suicide, especially by similar methods.

For loss survivors in particular, an increased attention on high-profile suicide deaths can cause a wide range of emotions.

For me, a description of method that is the same as how my sister died can cause various physical reactions and thoughts that I otherwise no longer have to face on a daily basis. Because people will often post comments on articles or social media platforms about celebrity suicide deaths, I might come across opinions that cause me additional pain. I may bristle, for example, at insensitive opinions or hateful comments directed to those who died by suicide. I know my experience is not unique; many of us who have been affected by suicide loss feel similarly about the emotional tumult caused by overwhelming media coverage.

On days where the media reporting is incessant, I have to protect myself more than I otherwise do. I will avoid most social and news media. I might need to carve out space at work to find some time alone, to breathe or listen to an upbeat song that helps me re-center. I dedicate time in the evening to return to my emotions and actively process them. I might also need to distract myself from the pain by watching silly television shows, or by indulging in retail therapy. I also try to eat as well as possible, stay hydrated, get natural light, and maintain good sleep hygiene. I also find myself reaching out to other suicide loss survivors on these days in order to share the heightened emotions and so that we can hold each other, even across wide distances, while we try to manage to get through these days as best as possible. I am grateful to have friends and family who alert me to articles and blogs that could be especially painful, so that I am less likely to come across them in the middle of a work day, where I do not want to fall into the spiral of re-opened grief.

Of course, some of the media coverage is positive, especially when it offers support to those who are struggling. If someone is feeling suicidal, we want the person to feel supported and loved in a decision to keep living. In the end, what rings truest for me is that our work is *to make people's lives worth living.* All people are worthy of living lives free from suicidal despair. Media coverage that shares this message can help the readers, viewers, or listeners feel supported.

We do not want to cause further pain to those of us who are already dealing with intense grief, loss, and traumatic memories.

To that end, the essays in this book do not describe methods of suicide death, suicide attempts, or self-harm, in alignment with feedback from other suicide loss survivors as well as information from reportingonsuicide.org. The essays in *Still With Us: Voices of Sibling Suicide Loss Survivors* emphasize messages of compassion and empathy and hope, of supportive families, friends, and communities, and of how sibling survivors can continue to live with memories of our loved ones by our sides.

Why people die by suicide

Part of my initial grieving process was to research suicide. Because I could not ask my sister what brought her to her final act, I turned to some of the leading researchers in suicidology to learn more about the topic. I wanted to know all that I could about why it is that some people die by suicide, but that the majority of people who have thoughts of suicide and struggle, even for years or decades with chronic suicidality, do not die by suicide. Why was my sister—why am I, as a loss survivor?—one of the unlucky ones? Understanding suicide at this level may or may not be helpful to you, but in case it might be, I recommend the book *Why People Die By Suicide* (2001) by Thomas Joiner. There are also many other wonderful books, documentaries, blogs, and articles that have been published on suicide, on surviving suicidal thoughts and/or attempts, and on suicide loss. I have included a list of books and articles specific to sibling suicide loss at the end of the book.

On support groups

Many of us will find that there is a benefit to attending a support group specific to suicide loss. For each suicide, the data estimate that an average of 135 people are exposed to the death, which results in 5.5 million U.S.A. residents who are exposed to suicide in a given 12-month period (Cerel, et. al., p. 4). With this statistic, one might imagine that there is always a suicide loss support group close by, but that may not always be the reality. If you are thinking about attending a suicide loss support group and are having difficulty locating one through your own contacts and communities, the American Foundation for Suicide Prevention's website (www.AFSP.org) maintains a list of suicide loss support groups in your area. Some areas might not (yet) have a support group dedicated specifically to suicide loss; in that case, a more general grief support group might offer similar benefits. What is important, I think, is to remember that a support group might be the right thing for you at this moment, or it might not be. You might decide to attend a support group and realize that you are not ready. You might never go to one. You might go on and off for many years. The decision of whether or not to attend a support group is a deeply personal one.

For me, finding help online has been beneficial. Connecting through social media with other sibling survivors of suicide loss has been one of the main ways that I have found to survive my sister's death. In the early months and years after my sister's death, I found my thoughts spinning in the late night hours or early morning hours. Being able to post on a Facebook group page about my thoughts, fears, and endless questions and then to receive responses almost immediately was a tremendous help. I have met many amazing survivors through online groups, some of whom I have later met in person (always by meeting in a public area first). Twitter has also been a helpful platform to connect with other loss survivors. Indeed, some of the survivors I have met online are also authors in this collection!

Online support groups can also be beneficial to those whose work schedules or other personal situations might inhibit attending in-person support groups. However, sometimes online support groups are less moderated than in-person support groups, and some posts and images can be triggering. Again, this might be a venue for you to explore, or you might prefer not to use online platforms for grief support. There are numerous resources out there, if you decide you would like to search for one (or some) that work best for you.

My sister Danielle

As I wrote the first draft of this introduction, I was five years into my grief of losing my younger sister and only sibling Danielle to suicide. My journey since my sister died has been complicated and predicated on my survival through the enormity of my grief.

Danielle died when I was 27 years old. Her death came two weeks after we celebrated her 24th birthday. Danielle was "my person." She was my soulmate sister. Our identities were utterly intertwined, but we were also our individual selves, which was made heartbreakingly clear in that her traumatic experiences were hers alone, and I could not take them away from her to ease her pain. As close as we were, I could not relieve her of her traumatic memories and flashbacks that came along with her P.T.S.D. If I could have taken her burdens on, I would have.

I am often reluctant to try and describe how close Danielle and I were to those who did not know her or our relationship to one another. Words continue to fail me. How can I explain to those who never met the two of us that Danielle was the other half of my heart? That every memory I have is somehow linked to her? That I only knew myself as an extension of her? That, although she was three-and-a-half years younger, she was the brave leader, the adventure-seeker, the risk-taker who paved the way for me to follow? She was amazing, intelligent, driven, compassionate, musical, empathetic, compassionate, and absolutely hilarious, with wit that could be dry, sarcastic, or silly.

I could get lost in describing our entwined lives, our sisterhood, or the multiple traumas my sister experienced that led to her terrible P.T.S.D. and eventually contributed in great part to her death by suicide. If you are reading this and know the pain of losing a sibling or a loved one to suicide, you too may have a deep and complex relationship to the person you miss and to the world you must now face without your person physically by your side.

In the moments after my sister's death, I did not know how I would survive the next few hours or days. After wading through the shock of the first few days of her death, I had no idea how to survive the next week, or, unimaginably, the next month. Thinking about the multiple months ahead, much less the years, decades, even a lifetime, was impossible. I closely followed the motto: "one day at a time." (On some days, especially in the beginning, the motto was "one hour at a time.") Somehow, those hours and days turned into weeks and months. Eventually, I made it through one year, and then multiple years. And here I am—still unable to envision the next big block of time (a decade?), but I continue to move forward, one step at a time. I continue to survive my sister's suicide. There is no timeline to grief and to grieving, and the timelines that some people have tried to push on me have never made sense. I will grieve my sister forever; she was a part of me, and she will forever be a part of me. I know that she is, and will always be, still with me.

I dedicate this compilation to my sister Danielle, to all the siblings who are honored in the following pages, and to your siblings, too. May we continue to find a way forward, even when our hearts are broken, and when we feel lost in our grief.

References:

Cerel, J., Brown, M. M., Maple, M., Singleton, M., Venne, J. V., Moore, M., & Flaherty, C. (2018). How Many People Are Exposed to Suicide? Not Six. *Suicide and Life-Threatening Behavior*, 1-6.

Halous DeSousa, M. (2012). *The forgotten mourners: Sibling survivors of suicide*. Outskirts Press.

Joiner, T. E. (2007). *Why people die by suicide*. Cambridge, MA: Harvard University Press.

Linn-Gust, M. (2001). *Do they have bad days in Heaven? Surviving the suicide loss of a sibling*. Roswell, GA: Balton Press Atlanta.

Wray, T. J. (2003). *Surviving the death of a sibling: Living through grief when an adult brother or sister dies*. New York, NY: Three Rivers Press.

On Being a Sibling Suicide Loss Survivor

by Lena Heilmann

Although there are many similarities in how we grieve our siblings lost to suicide, there is no one way to grieve. Grief is personal, complex, and not bound to any specific timeframe. Below are sentences that have provided me comfort over the years. Some of these sentences are ones I came across in my grieving process; others have come out of my own grief.

I encourage you to add phrases that are not on this list, highlight phrases that resonate with you, and cross off whatever does not speak to you.

- Grief is just another word for love with no place to go.
- I hurt so much because I loved her so much.
- This is a hard journey; I don't think it can be otherwise.
- My grieving is an expression of the love I continue to feel.
- It is okay to feel happy and joyous after my sibling's suicide; I have the right to feel however I feel.
- It is okay for me to say no to attending events that will be too overwhelming for me.
- It is okay for me to set firm boundaries and hold them. Others who have not been through this loss might not understand the depths of my pain, but they need to respect my boundaries.
- It is okay to cry for no reason. It's okay to cry for every reason.
- It is okay to have conflicting emotions.
- It is okay to have better days. It is okay to have worse days. It is okay just to have days.

- It is okay to have energy and to want to fix the world.
- It is okay to be tired. So very tired.
- There is no timeline for grief. As long as I am living, I will be grieving my sibling.

I

The First Five Years of Grief

Retail Therapy and the Process of Mourning

by Lena Heilmann

[I wrote this piece four months after my sister's death.]

In 2003, during spring of our senior year of high school, my closest friend E's father died as a result of cancer. On the day that he passed, E and I went to a shopping mall, and we spent the day deciding between the available options of shirts, skirts, shoes, and tops. Our conversation during that shopping trip focused solely on whether or not the green shirt was the right shade of green, or whether the tan shoes had too high of a heel.

In the days and weeks following this trip, I often wondered why the first thing E and I did was to go shopping. Why did we turn to retail therapy as a way to cope with grief? What were we seeking?

I think what we were searching for was a feeling of control in a world that we felt was out of control. The thousands of snap decisions we made that day helped overcome that feeling of helplessness that threatened to overwhelm us. A relief to the big questions—why E's father? why now, just a few weeks before high school graduation?—the decisions we made while shopping allowed us to know answers to minute questions: yes, the green shirt goes well your jeans, and the tan shoes are definitely not too high. Those tiny, unimportant decisions gave us back some semblance of control, and we could walk away with tangible proof that we still had some say in life's decisions, even if they were of the most trivial sort.

Recently, I returned to retail therapy as a way of coping with grief. The day before Thanksgiving, my sister ended her life, and I, alongside my parents, held her as she died in the hospital Thanksgiving Day.

It's been four months since she passed, and I still cannot confront the grief directly or the idea of a future without her. To say she was my best friend is an understatement; in fact, all words pertaining to our relationship will always be an understatement, so I will not even attempt to write them here.

We planned a beautiful funeral for my sister. For one week, I was engrossed in details that kept me breathing between the moments where I had to succumb to the pain and impossibility of losing my sister only two weeks after we celebrated her 24th birthday. I spent tens of hours on her funeral program, choosing a perfect photo for her obituary, discussing flower arrangements, and planning the words I would say during the ceremony.

I also became fixated on what to wear to the funeral. My sister and I often went shopping together, and I reconciled our habitual spending of money with, again, the idea of control through retail therapy. Shopping was an escape from my sister's P.T.S.D., from her panic attacks, and from a life that kept forcing obstacles and trauma upon her. We both regained momentary control in our decisions in those moments when we discussed whether or not she needed a sundress, and, in that moment, we could imagine a future in which that sundress would be worn on a carefree summer day, the breeziness of the fabric complementing my sister's breeziness in demeanor and spirit. Maybe it all sounds trivial, but my sister and I watched her pain destroy and ultimately kill her, and shopping gave us access to moments of control and escape through these small hopeful decisions.

On the days leading up to my sister's funeral, I scoured the Internet, searching for a dress to wear. Friends, neighbors, and family surrounded me and my parents, supporting our every step. I was not alone while I searched for the perfect dress for my sister's funeral. I found a beautiful one: it was mostly black, with a gray section overlaid with black lace down one side. I couldn't afford it at its current price, but my then-partner mentioned it to a close family friend, and she bought it for me. While the planning for the first dress was underway, my dearest friend and her mom went shopping for me and found a dark blue, crushed velvet dress with 3/4 sleeves. I spent hours deliberating which dress to wear, when I realized that I could do a change of clothing: one dress for the funeral, and one for the reception at our house to follow. The idea was completely ludicrous—I knew this then, and I know this now. But it was also perfect. It was the kind of decision my sister would have whole-heartedly supported, and it would have been another of millions of inside jokes. So I decided for the outfit change.

Once I had the dress(es), I had to focus on accessories. I imagined contrasting the black, dark blue, and grays with bright red. For her 24th birthday, I went with my sister to get our nails done. She always chose a deep or bright purple or red. I can hardly bring myself to wear clear nail polish, but on that day I chose a light pink. My sister and I joked that one day, in the distant future, I too could wear the bright colors she wore with confidence. To contrast the funeral dress, then, I decided to wear bright red nail polish, for the first time in my life. The red nails then became the basis for all other accessories—a red barrette my friend and her mom bought me, red post earrings that arrived the day of the funeral, so that I could only wear them with the second dress, and, finally, bright red gloves that exposed my painted fingernails.

The night before the funeral, I tried to complete my outfit. I still needed the gloves, and the earrings hadn't arrived by then. So, off I went to chain stores in the area, accompanied by: my then-partner, a BFF, my cousin and his girlfriend, my mother's dear friend, my friend whose father passed away our senior year of high school, and her husband. This group helped me to shop. We made a contest of who could find the most appropriate red earrings, and, although I didn't end up buying any in the end, I was, for a few hours, focused on the most trivial of decisions. I had control, the option of saying "no," in the face of a future I could not deny and choose to change. I had no control over my sister's final decision, but I could make infinite infinitely small decisions.

The final touches for my funeral outfit were a pair of my sister's black heels (we have the same large foot size) and her black and white scarf with details in blue and—yes—bright red.

In the end, my outfits were perfect and the funeral absolutely beautiful.

But my life is ultimately shattered.

And still I have to go through each day with the knowledge that I will never hold my sister in my arms again, that I will never hear her laugh except for maybe on saved voice mail messages I cannot bring myself to listen to yet, or that I will never hear her breathing in her sleep, knowing she was, at that moment, safe.

From all the people who have reached out to me and offered to me their own methods of dealing with the death of a loved one, or from the books I have read and websites I've skimmed, I've learned that there is no one way of dealing with grief. Each moment is utterly different from the next, and while the trivial can expand to become indispensable, other stressors (trying to finish my Ph.D., maintaining a relationship) are mitigated.

Retail therapy is reality therapy. I have to try to survive my sister's suicide, and although I might not know what I am doing, I am trying to give myself space to breathe in such a way that my sister's memory can breathe with me, breaths of joy and permission to enjoy the more trivial and playful moments of life.

King Stephen

by Sarah Jolly

Steve died ten months ago. He died as a result of an accident during a psychotic episode. He was 22.

I start with this for two reasons; one, whenever I talk about Steve, I do not want his death to be the last part of the conversation. Two, if you are anything like me, when you hear that someone has died, you want to know the details. And that's OK. I like talking about Steve, and I do not mind talking about the way he died. Now that I am a part of this world of grieving, I notice that people do not know how or if to bring up the person who died, or their death. I hear "I do not know what to say" a lot, and my response is, "That's OK, I do not know what to say either." It's awkward, and it's awkward for me, too. But that should not stop you from talking about your sibling if you want to. The big takeaway here is to talk about your sibling in exactly the way you want. Trying to cater to pressure from anyone else or any societal norms can add to the stress and sadness.

I have two more siblings: an older sister and another younger brother (Steve's twin). Although we have the most similar experience, we all grieve differently, so remember that any advice I give here may only be uniquely for me.

Ten months later, and Steve is still all that I think about. He's always there. It does not matter what I am doing or who I am with. Nothing makes me feel better. Music that I used to love is not good anymore, and I cannot connect to people as closely. People say it gets better with time. It does not feel that way, it feels the opposite—every day is another day that he's not here. I miss him more every day because he's not here to alleviate that desire to see him and spend time with him.

You might experience what I call "the fog." I had no idea I was in the fog until I felt it lift for the first time, about eight months after he died. I only realized the fog had lifted once I was talking to and interacting with people like I used to, when Steve was still alive. The dissipation lasted about a week. Once you've been out of the fog it's easier to see when you are back in it. The fog means I do not remember entire conversations with people. I feel more distracted. I went to a newly bereaved grief group, and I did find that helpful, because they taught that things such as feeling like you are experiencing the symptoms of your loved one's illness are normal. You are okay to be sad, feel like you are struggling with your own mental health like seeing shadows and not being able to connect with people. It's okay to not be happy.

I hate that he's not out in the world right not representing himself. He's not making new friends at the gym or making idle conversation with the grocery store clerk. I feel like it's my responsibility to keep him present since he cannot do it himself. So I bring him up constantly. I got my first tattoo on my right forearm so it's the first thing people see when they shake my hand, and I can introduce him. It does not feel sufficient, but it helps. It helps me to know that I have a really good group of support and people in my life that I can talk about Steve as much as I want.

I hate that I cannot be stronger for him. When he first died, I wanted to use him as my motivation. I wanted to get fitter, lose weight, crush my job, stay in school and get good grades, for Steve. It did not happen that way. I took a year off school, and it was absolutely, without question, the right decision. Sometimes it feels like I'm using the death of my brother as an excuse to slack off, but it's just not true. Grief is a full-time job and takes all of your mental energy. Taking time off is crucial because it gives your mind a break from your other full-time obligations. It hurts to think that I have to live the rest of my life without him. But it does encourage me that I have the rest of my life to succeed for him. It does not all have to happen right now.

What I hate the most is that he had such big plans, and he died without accomplishing them. He wanted to be a big successful businessman. He wanted to be the next Berkshire

Hathaway guy. It feels daunting to embark on this journey, but I do think that if I can accomplish some of these plans, then that will finally be enough.

Steve loved to work out, so I have been enjoying working out a lot more to feel closer to him. I set a goal when he died to run a half marathon in less than two hours by the end of the year, which I was able to accomplish on December 15. Now I've signed up for my first ever marathon. Steve wanted to be big and important, so I want to do that for him. I've created my first ever BHAG: Big Hairy Audacious Goal. I've never really made big future goals before, but I want to do this for Steve. I hope to get his name on something big—like a business or psychology school. It's definitely a BHAG, but it helps because I feel like I have something to work on for the rest of my life to bring me closer to him.

And Then, She Was Gone

by Elliat Graney-Saucke

The best way I can describe it is that the chemistry in my body changed. All of my insides rearranged themselves, had to, in order to appropriately respond and reflect the new reality I was forced to deal with. But I say that it was my body that changed, because it was on such a deep, foundational, gut level. I knew nothing would ever be the same, that I was changed and a new person in so many ways I had yet to comprehend.

I lost my younger sister a little over one year ago. We were 2.5 years apart in age—my baby sister (always), and I was her big sister. There were lots of typical dynamics in this: sibling rivalry, competition, protectiveness, mentoring and advice, and the eternal and necessary conversation and comradery of being each other's confidants around the ways our parents drove us nuts. We were very different as well, and we fought a lot, especially in middle school. She stole my prized makeup and magazines and clothes, which looking back was her actually admiring me, but at the time was infuriating. She got away with it because of her innocent face in my mom's eyes, and her new ability to lie well. We moved beyond that, and she always turned to me when she really needed help, when things got really hard. Throughout our relationship we had ridiculously stupid and fabulous humor together as well, which is one of the traits I remember constantly. What a goofball.

This first year has been unreal, surreal, dazed, stunned … It has taken everything in me to allow myself to move between letting myself cry deep and heavy, feeling hopelessly bereaved, to inevitably moving back into the required functionality of everyday life. I have still needed to work and feed myself and stay functional in order to survive. I have moved through shock, to care-taking other family and organizing memorials, to being shut down depressed, to aching with missing her and crying hysterically, to numbed out and feeling like I should be feeling more, feeling guilty on so many levels, and of course the fantasies that I think will never end but only subside of what I could have done to save her, to rescue her from all the distress and pain and just keep her safe, keep her safe like I was supposed to as her protector and confidant, as her older sister.

But suicide is f*cked … On one hand, you have to face the reality of what has happened, that the one person who was witness to your childhood, who had nicknames for you because they couldn't say your name right as a baby, that this person is gone. So what do you do, accept it? But it's not okay! It's really, really not okay! The pain caused by this person being taken from you, that an actual part of you had been nonconsensually ripped out from your arms, your life, your insides, that you can never call on the phone again to say, "Hi, I love you and am thinking of you," that you can't smell their hair or hold their hand … How are you ever supposed to accept that? How? And yet, what choice do you have? What are you supposed to do with all the people who are messaging you, all the people who, when they see you, say they are so sorry and hold your arm or hug you, when it feels like they want something from you or to give you something that only muffles the feelings. All the times when you start getting ready for bed and take the trash out and go into a sort of neutral mode, only to be rudely shocked back into the reality that something bad has just happened, that your sister is dead … But how can that be reality? How can that be true? But, it is. And that is the truth you have to sit with. You have to let your body digest and ingest the fact that something terrible has happened, that you have lost something, that death has occurred. And my sister wasn't taken from me by cancer or something else I can be angry at, but I have the distinct impression that suicide is a whole other beast. Because her death feels like a violation on another level, that she was in so much pain that she felt this was her best option. I don't accept it. And then, you come back again to the fact that this is the reality, this has happened, and so, as f*cked up as it is, on some level you must accept this version of events, because there is no choice, and she is gone now.

There are so many things that I wish. I wish I had been able to save my sister. I can't express to you how badly I want this, how much I wanted it for years and years leading up to her death. I wanted independence and empowerment for my sister; I wanted her to have the same kind of community I found when I came out and gained my queer family/community. I wanted her to have a loving partner who lifted her up and supported her healing, for her to have her own home and get out of the cycle of being an adult teenager. I wanted her to get sober and deal with her addiction and to get the healing and love and support she needed to work through her trauma. I talked her through some extremely painful situations, listened while she cried about feeling so bad about where her life was at, that at 30 she felt like she had not amounted to anything, surrounded by a family of ambitious women. While I cooked her breakfast and massaged her feet, watched her sleep and laughed with her on the rare occasions we saw each other, when she could be present with me, it was complicated and sometimes felt like looking down into a vast chasm of more than I knew what to do with.

As a cultural organizer, filmmaker, and artist, I help tell stories of individuals and communities. I care a lot about other people and what kind of world we live in. It is my life's work to communicate different lived realities and try to make the world a better place. And I didn't know how to save my sister. Some of her choices also were not good for me to be around, and I had to find ways to protect myself, to struggle with her patterns and choices and break away myself to build my own adult life. Is it selfish to not sacrifice yourself to save someone else? I thought I could role model and lead the way, setting boundaries as a healthy way to have a relationship. I always was so jealous of people who had a peer relationship with their siblings, being able to share their lives together. I wanted that for both of us so badly

… I would get mad and be judgmental about where she was at in her life and her functionality, wanting to share my accolades and adventures and relationship problems with her. It got better in the end. We got more of that closeness somehow, which I am grateful for, but it is hard when your successes become a weapon of self-defeat in the life of someone you love. I came to realize that all she needed from me was my love, and the best we could do was just to love each other. My loving her and telling her this, while admitting to having been judgmental in the past, letting go of this judgment and owning that this was my own stuff and not fair, allowed her to open up, to trust me more and to tell me some of her truths that she had never shared. It allowed us to have a truer connection.

The last time we really spent time together, she talked for days about all these horrible things, and I knew she wasn't talking to anyone else, so I took it all in. I took her to a bookshop and got her a nice notebook and told her to write out all the bad things. We talked about how toxic and bad it was for her to keep all those things to herself, and if there was no one to talk to, at least she could write it out. A few months later, she told me the journaling had turned into a memoir she was writing, that once she opened the tap, it kept going and wouldn't stop. Our love gave her enough trust in me that she was able to open up and write, to trust herself enough to tell her story. I am still so proud of her. And it is the memoir that is one main thing she left me when she took her life. Something I still can't fully process, because it is so huge, so huge. An honor, and in ways, a burden, that is so heavy to carry. My sister is gone, and I have her memoir, a suitcase of some of her clothes, before the rest were donated away, paperwork I found in her room, and odd trinkets. I've realized that this is our last dance; the memoir is our last artistic collaboration with her music and illustrations, her stories and my stories, our memories from the past and the future mixed together somehow. Lost in time. But I will be giving myself as many years, decades if I need, my lifetime if I need, to handle it. Her story is so huge, and my heart is still too broken to read about her heartbreak. It will take a community of people who help me through that when I reach that crossing. But she wrote it, and I am so, so proud of her.

I keep thinking of how to explain my grief process, and all there is this mess of words and feelings. I go to therapy once a week, and I go to acupuncture and take care of my body as best I can. I deal with my migraines, skin problems, and anxiety from emotional stress. I try to build myself back up with my amazing community of friends, to reconnect with my passion and ambition so I can still have a career and not feel defeated by all the heaviness. My relationship with my parents has changed greatly too, so I see and talk to them more now. It has taken me a year to feel like I can even see where I am, and I don't think I'm even really there. Somewhere? I have struggled with everyone in my family having radically different ways of grieving and processing the pain of her loss. I have struggled with my role in my family, of being a caretaker and not always getting the support I needed. I have kept myself busy as usual with my dozens of projects. I have lost old friends who couldn't deal with my grief and loss and who wanted to pretend that nothing had happened or go back to business as usual.

When you lose a sibling to suicide, a part of your childhood and innocence is taken from you. It ages you, significantly, because you are that much closer to mortality for yourself and the rest of your immediate family, and you have no more tolerance for bullshit or people who feel uncomfortable with your pain. The best advice I got was from a friend in Germany: my job was to grieve, that I had to do nothing else, for a year, longer, that all the people needing things from me and not understanding or empathizing with my world being upside down were of no concern and to let go of all expectation for myself to do anything except to be in my feelings and get comfort and love and support from friends and community and healers. I saw a spiritual guide who connected with the energy of my sister, and whether or not that is for you is not the point here, because the important thing was that she said my sister had realized she had messed up and didn't realize she was going to hurt so many people she loved. I didn't realize until I heard those words how much I needed to hear something from the other side of all this, that I was struggling so deeply with this being a one-sided transition / conversation / action. I needed to be able to be angry at her for leaving me, for hurting me, and not being able to ever say goodbye, not ever being able to see her again.

I still feel like I should be going to support groups for those who survive losing others to suicide, but even the notebook I have specifically for my sister I can hardly write in. I am afraid that if I let myself sit too long in the sadness that it will consume me, that I won't be able to survive in this world, that I won't be able to get up again. So I have her picture as the center of my altar. I acknowledge and see her every day, and some days it aches inside me, and I can't really face the full feeling of her being gone, and other days I see her face and remember her and feel her close, and other days she is just there with me.

There is nothing like the loss of a sibling to suicide, and you will never be the same again. This is just true. And it is also so important to know that you are strong and that feeling sad and mourning in the ways that you need to is also the strong and brave thing to do. While we live in a busy rat race world that does not want to slow down for your devastation, you have to force that space for yourself if you want to not have this rip you apart. In the Western world / U.S., we sadly live in a culture that does not fully grant us a healthy relationship with death, pushing elders and the sick away into facilities so we don't see the full cycle of life. I have lost friends to suicide and car crashes, which is not the same by a long shot to what it has been to lose a sibling, but with all of these losses, I am left with the same resounding truth that we do not all have the privilege of getting old, and so for those who are not with us anymore, it is our duty and responsibility to live our lives as fully and with as much integrity as possible. I want to live the best life I can, to do work I am good at and that is valuable, to love fully and to be witness to and present in the world, because I am here and I can.

I live my best life for myself, but also for my sister, and because she is not here anymore to live her life, I am going to live for both of us. Taking moments when I go out for a walk, breathing the air, looking around at nature and the birds, and noticing. And saying to myself, I am grateful to be alive.

My Journey in my "New Normal" Without my Little Brother

by Helio Nowell

This December 27th, 2018 will be two years since his passing … I still don't know how to act. My then-fiancée (and now wife) and I went out on a date to see *Jackie*, the movie about the wife of JFK and her version of her husband's death. We left the theater and began our drive home. I remember telling my wife, "It must be awful one morning kissing your husband and that same night planning his funeral." No more than 20 minutes after saying that, my phone rings, and it's my dad. The call that would forever change my life.

Dad said, "I need you to go home and go be with your mom. Your brother is in the hospital." I got home, and Mom had no idea. I hugged my mom and told her, "Pablo is in the hospital and Dad will call us." My sister's then-boyfriend walked in (he's an ER nurse), and he said, "I am so sorry …" My mom collapsed, and I caught her. She began praying and praising God for my brother's life. I lost it and broke down.

I spoke to my brother the night before and told him how much I loved him and missed him. He lived in Salem, OR with his wife and daughter. The next day he was gone. It was the loneliest day of my life. That night my brother visited me in my dreams. He was smiling like I've never seen him smile. He told me he was okay and happy. He told me the next few days would suck, but I needed to tell people his story and live for him. He looked at his watch, and he said, "I love you. I have to go." I begged my brother not to leave me, but he kept walking. My life now has a massive void. I find myself wanting to text him and tell him I love him and miss him. I hate not hearing his voice. I miss my best friend.

Since his passing, on his birthday (he's had two thus far), we honor him and share our favorite memory of my brother. We then release balloons into the sky in hopes they can touch the sky and touch him. I have started a small foundation to honor him and hopes to end this horrible illness and save someone's life. I wear his bracelet daily, and his picture is on my desk.

Dealing with grief is the most exhausting thing I have ever done. One second I am happy, the next I am crying, the next I am angry, and so on … It's like a ball of rubber bands. All of the bands are a feeling. All into one ball. I have turned to God more than anything for comfort and giving Him my pain. Without Him, I would be way lost. I have also began working out more to release my pain on something healthy. I turned away from alcohol. I have and still go to counseling to talk about my feelings.

The first year was a fog. Just a mess. But the second year has sucked more. It has been the hardest thus far, and I pray that it doesn't get any worse. The pain and grief is overwhelming, and I find myself dreaming of my little brother almost nightly … I feel lost at times. I am happy most of the time. Losing my brother, identifying him, leading worship at his funerals, and laying him to rest have been the hardest. Living without him is the worst. My wife and I are expecting our son, and I have a feeling he will be born around the time of my brother's anniversary, which wouldn't surprise me, knowing my brother's sense of humor is insane, lol. This will be a reminder that he lives through my baby boy and through all of us.

Although my brother is no longer on Earth, I believe his soul is eternal and lives in us, and all around us. He is in Heaven with His creator, and I will forever live for my little brother. I love him, and he is my hero.

The Cake

by Barb Kulka

In our family, food is love. And in our family, a birthday cake is a thing. Not just any old cake, but an old-fashioned, homemade chocolate cake. The recipe is fairly standard, and it was shared with my mother in the early ’60s. Pretty much every birthday since then we have had The Cake.

There are only two variations to The Cake: with jam in between the layers or not. And each of us has our preference. The secret to this delicious moist cake is to make it a week ahead of time and put it in the freezer and ice it with rich chocolate icing after it thaws.

The Cake has been made far and wide as my father was in the military, and we traveled across Canada and Europe while our little family of four children was growing up.

The Cake continued to be made for grandchildren and then great-grandchildren. As time went on, some wanted something different, but my brother and I remained loyal and in love with the jam-filled Cake.

For my brother’s memorial service, we put together a slideshow of pictures of his life. In the early years it was mostly birthday pictures, and The Cake remained a constant in a lot of the pictures. Even his obituary picture was a picture of him at a recent birthday. Unfortunately, we had to cut The Cake out of the picture, but the friends and family who loved him best knew The Cake was there!

On the first birthday after his death, a friend texted me and said, “I hope someone somewhere made a cake today.” And I’m thinking, that's how we go on … by keeping the traditions we have made and passing them down and making The Cake for our friends and family.

Brian, wherever you are, I hope you're enjoying a piece of your jam-filled cake every year on your birthday!

II

Grieving Years Five Through Ten

Looking For You

by Sarah, age 28, survivor of 5 ¼ years

"I'm setting sail, on a whale.
I majestically set out to sea.
Look out below, all you fishes.
My blow hole's about to blow.
I'm moving on, with this song...
I'm moving on.
And as I ride that whale,
I can't help but think of unkind memories.
Let them sink into the sea,
as the wind, the breeze, blows upon me."
~TimE.

My brother died on a cold night in late October. He was 21 years and three weeks old. My life and heart would be forever changed. I dropped everything and moved home.

Tim was a gifted guitarist and singer-songwriter. He left no note, said no goodbyes, but just weeks before his death, he completed an original album of music.

I spent the first winter after Tim's death mostly in bed, hiding beneath the covers, reading spiritual texts. While journaling, I wrote, "I am always just looking for you." Since then, the phrase has continued to echo in my head.

I am always just looking for you.

Once over coffee, a friend asked, "Do you think about him every day?" I was shocked at the question.

No, not every day. I think of him with every breath. It's a knife to the heart, a punch to the gut, gnashing of the teeth, a silent scream. That pain is the price of my love and memories of my brother.

My mother said to me, "Every day, I cry invisible tears."

I still see flashes of that October night in my father's eyes. It was my father who found him that night, too late. His only son. Our nightmare realized.

"We're drifting in the universe,
when worst comes to worst.
We'll find our place
in time and space..."

Carlos Castaneda wrote, "We either make ourselves miserable, or we make ourselves strong. The amount of work is the same." I have done my share of each.

I'm learning the hard way that denying emotions by drinking alcohol, overeating, or smoking, ultimately makes me feel worse—no matter how many times I try.

What has helped is exercise, eating healthily and regularly, staying hydrated, tea, hot baths and saunas, being out in nature, sunshine, breathwork, healing touch/bodywork, singing. I adopted a rescue puppy. She is loving, joyful, lives in-the-moment, and it rubs off on her humans. I am forever grateful to my sweet little panda bear. She can cheer me up no matter what.

"In with positivity,
out with negativity.
Bust down the walls,
try not to fall."

After Tim's death, out of both love and desperation, I began to learn to play chords on his guitar. I have been surprised and grateful to discover my own passion and gifts for music, singing, and songwriting. It feels like a way to keep him alive, a way to channel his spirit. It is keeping me alive, too.

In the Lakota tradition, a person suffering great loss and grieving deeply is considered "the most holy," and closest to God. Their prayers are considered especially powerful, and they are often asked to pray on the behalf of others.

In Hawaiian there's a word meaning total forgiveness: *Ho'oponopono*.

A translation I learned is: I'm so sorry, I love you, please forgive me, I thank you.

"Have a little faith.
Keep it up, keep pace.
Don't have time to waste..."

Along the way, friends have offered me advice and consolation. One suggested, "Forgiveness is giving up all hope of having a better past." Another offered the words of Christ: "Let not your heart be troubled." One said, "In Heaven there's a place called the Temple of Voices, and your brother is up there jamming with Hendrix and all the greats!"

It could be true, but I'm still here looking for you.

I've looked in the darkest, ugliest places, believing death to be something dark and ugly.

I've looked in every face I've met, in every sunset, in every song I hear on the radio, in every star in the sky.

I've learned that I don't have to search the darkness. I can look in the breeze, in the bird's song, in the ocean wave, in the late afternoon light.

To honor Tim's life, as well as his death, I feel the need to share his story. After he died, I began to study documentary film. One day, I will make a film for Tim.

Music is one of my brother's most profound and powerful gifts to me. By going forth in his place, I believe that I can heal myself and others with music. In this way I hope to spread Tim's love and light into the world.

I am always just looking for you.

"Words can't express how much I love you...
So maybe If I put it in song,
we can move on,
because our love
will keep us above
forever."
~TimE.

I wish I could hug my brother; hear him sing.
Timmy, I will always be looking for you.

After Five Years

by Amy Thrasher

The first months were a dark blur. There was the dark depth of sleep, and more sleep, and every time I woke up, the wall of harsh awareness struck me down. And when I was awake, there was the constant blinking on and off of blaring recognition that she was gone. I would have a moment's reprieve as brief as a glance, and then the truth hit broadside again, and I capsized. I slept as much as I could.

She was my older sister, eight years older. She took care of me when I was little, changed my diapers. She loved frogs. She sewed clothes for my Barbie dolls. She took me to stage crew when she was in high school and I was her kid sister. All my teachers thought I would be a good student because she had been excellent. She was always on the lookout for me, deeply generous. She was a computer network engineer with a mathematical brain, a master of 1000 piece puzzles, and shy but strong. She was a sailor, and won Hobie Cat races on the weekends. Everyone knew her by her smile. When her mind gave out, and she could no longer be in the regular business world full-time, she devoted herself to her art. She became a quilt artist and developed new techniques of embellishment. She encouraged others and connected people within that art sphere.

My parents were despondent. My brother, gutted. My husband held me, and I held my dog, and we held on tight. My in-laws surrounded us with love and understanding, and food to keep us going.

I knew I had to keep working and do what I knew how to do through sheer mechanical routine. I asked for part-time medical leave, so that I could avoid the types of tasks that required new thought, because I had nothing to give, nothing that would support the generation of new ideas and plans. I could only take a step, and then another step, because that's what my legs knew to do. My mind felt disassembled, my heart pulverized.

For the first nine months, I cried every morning on my drive to work. I dressed bundled up, regardless of the weather, covering myself with layers, sweaters, and scarves. I wasn't cold, but I needed protection. My chest held a cavernous vacancy. I had to cover it up. I began to wear multiple rings, necklaces, and bracelets, seeking protection and self-preservation.

It is too simple to say I was profoundly sad. I was, but that doesn't suffice.

I was never angry with her. I knew her demons too well. Still, I had cauldrons of rage to spare.

- Towards the person who smiled on our walk to a lunch meeting and breezily said, "How are you?" It felt like an affront to the existence of my sister. How dare they ask, *how are you*?
- That anger burned on high toward those who lived near her but removed themselves emotionally across the years while her mental illness continued to magnify.
- Toward the mental health "system," which only a person with an acutely functioning brain could navigate, while my sister drifted away.
- Toward myself, for my blind belief that my sister would continue to survive. Once, when I asked about her depression and if she ever thought of suicide, she had told me, "No, just a vague sense of wishing for not being." And I had believed her.

I had wanted to believe her. I still want to believe her.

With her death all of the assumptions I had held about our relationship suddenly came into sharper focus.

- How she would be there and help guide my mother, brother, and me through my father's end of life.
- How she would be there to help me figure out financial planning, with her ease in solving mathematical puzzles.

- How, at some point when I finished my own career, we would create art together. That was the haziest of the assumptions, the furthest out.

In the place of these assumptions, there lay a dread sense of light extinguished.

Going to her house, going through her things, I gathered the art materials of hers that I could manage. Her jewelry carried her sense of delight in the beauty of the world. I made a collection of it.

Returning home, I used her art materials to make something for her, of her. I used her cloth from her quilting supplies, the watery blue one with a print reminiscent of a navigational map, and her embroidery thread and beads. I embroidered and painted the point of land we lived on as children, with a lighthouse and a compass. As I made it, I knew it wasn't very good, but that wasn't the point at all. I ended up throwing it away, and maybe that was the point after all. Then I used her green cloth with the gold ginkgo leaves printed on it and embroidered a tree frog, embellished with beads. This somehow seemed worthy. I hung it in my living room. It is still encouraging me.

I went to a therapist to help me through the first two years. At first, I could only talk for 20 minutes before I would be overcome with exhaustion. Slowly, slowly, I could talk longer. I began to talk through the hour. I agonized over why this happened and how this could have been prevented. I explored the possibility that some people's mental illness, like any ravaging illness, might go too far and become terminal.

People in my life revealed to me their own experiences of losing a sibling. I learned it is all too common. I read a few essays by sibling survivors. When I joined an online group for sibling survivors, I could hear and read my own loss in their comments, see my own bruised journey reflected. My rambling shards of discrepant thoughts and feelings were accepted there. And together, again and again, we all acknowledged the irony of not wanting anyone else to feel this excruciating loss, yet finding comfort in our own devastated company.

The cards and the care that once flowed from more distant friends and acquaintances eventually dried up. People have a way of letting others' pain dissipate from their everyday existence. At the time it seemed incomprehensible that others could just return to normal. Nothing seemed that it could ever be normal again. Now my circle of grief is much smaller. My husband, my in-laws, what is left of my family now that my sister and father have died, my friends who have lost siblings to suicide—we live with it.

I gradually worked through my anger. For me, the questioning why and the anger were all of one piece. As that agonized piece dissolved over time, I eventually felt freer.

I took to wearing at least one piece of her jewelry every day. I still do. She is with me always. And when people comment on the ring or the bracelet or the necklace, I say it was my sister's. Her love of beauty brings her into the conversation, with me. And whenever I begin to do a piece of art, whether it's just a sketch or a more ambitious project, I think of her.

My Soulmate Sister, Danielle

by Lena Heilmann

[Written in 2017]

I have been grappling with a fundamental question for over five years now, ever since the day that Danielle died by suicide. I constantly ask myself: what does it mean for me to be a sister, if the other half of that relationship is no longer alive? Can I still claim an identity as a sibling? What does it mean for me to be both a sister and a survivor of suicide loss?

I did not always see the point of separation between me and my sister; in my mind, we were part of a continuum; one being split into two bodies, meant to share this world together. When my sister Danielle died, I realized that part of me died with her, and part of her now lives on with me.

Our sibling relationship was fairly straightforward. Danielle and I shared biological parents, a childhood, and a young adulthood. We quarreled as children, but we were also fiercely protective of one another. We traveled together every summer from Colorado to Germany. We shared some of the same friends. Our conversations verged on parodies of the movie *Nell*. We had a sister language, suffixes attached to words; inside jokes built upon inside jokes; dark humor to address painful moments; a certain wiggle of the hand and chant to signify a "sister promise," the deepest and most honest promise we could make to one another. We loved each other the most.

When Danielle first died, no one overlooked my pain. Everyone in my life had witnessed our close sisterly bond; they acknowledged my devastation. In this way, I was lucky. However, when a new job opportunity in 2014 took me to Illinois, I only then started to experience the vast loneliness and misunderstanding of being a sibling survivor. Some people, of course, profoundly understood my loss. Others, however, had conversations that I before only knew anecdotally. A conversation began with my vulnerable sharing of how my sister died. The response: "Your poor parents. How utterly devastating for them. Losing a child is the worst pain someone can endure. You? You're young; you'll get over this and lead a normal life. How *are* your parents handling this?" I have learned to reply calmly that my parents and I—*we*—are all trying to do the best we can. Of *course* my parents' loss is horrific and tragic, but mine is, too. Instead of feeling comforted or acknowledged during those conversations, I felt overlooked, invisible, forgotten.

After Danielle died, I told my friends and family that I did not need to hear any particular words—I just wanted to be remembered. I asked those who cared for me to send me a heart emoji whenever they thought of me. I didn't need any special words; I did not want to be forgotten.

Being a sibling survivor of suicide loss is a complex and painful identity. I was three and a half when Danielle was born, so most of my earliest memories include her. My entire life was entangled with hers. She was genetically the person most similar to me. Danielle and I were supposed to grow old together; be aunts to one another's children; share responsibilities as our parents aged. All of that future we imagined is no longer available. I still survive—there is still love and beauty in this world—but my loss cannot be downplayed because I am "young" or not a parent, child, or spouse of the deceased.

After my sister's death, I did not know who shared a loss like my own. I was so grateful when a former friend of my sister's reached out to me. Just six months earlier, she had lost her very close cousin (they were raised together as siblings) to suicide. For the first time, I heard myself in someone else's voice. I realized I desperately needed to talk to other people who shared my loss. Another friend lost her sister traumatically, and, even though it was not a suicide death, there were close parallels that resonated deeply with me. Knowing that these two friends were finding their way through their grief allowed me, for the first time, to think that maybe, just maybe, I could, too. I was (and will forever be) so grateful to these two friends who reached out to me in the weeks after my sister's passing. They were the first people who showed me, by their sheer survival, that there are others who have walked these paths before me, and I can look toward their bravery and strength to continue to move forward.

Finding more sibling survivors of suicide loss around me was difficult. I traveled a lot, and my thoughts often kept me up in the lonely hours of deepest night. I eventually found much-needed solace, support, and companionship in online support groups specifically designated for sibling survivors of suicide. There, I found facets of my story appearing over and over again. This repetition and understanding was what I needed to survive.

Lessons learned, five years out

Over five years into my grief, I can identify some of the patterns of the year. My sister died in November; the fall and winter are now my hardest seasons. Grief is closer to me in these months—it surrounds me like static—invisible to see as a force, but I can feel its energy all the time. Spring and summer are lighter seasons—the days are longer, and I have more energy. Grief is less immediate, but it is more likely to catch me off-guard when listening to a song or catching a specific scent I associate with my sister. The earthquakes of grief appear without warning, and I am less prepared to weather them.

I have learned to make space for my grief. I cannot ignore it or push it aside. If I am in a place where I cannot address my grief with an open heart, I find a place for it to set aside temporarily and promise myself I will return to it that night. I keep my promise to myself.

I continue to go to therapy. Immediately after Danielle died, I went to therapy twice a week, sometimes more. My reality had been so completely shattered that I did not recognize myself in the mirror. My brain worked on overdrive to figure out how I could negotiate with Death to bring my sister back. I would have done anything, and I wanted to try everything.

Surviving the first year of my grief was endlessly difficult. I felt completely unmoored, and each day could bring any range of emotions. Getting through each month, each season without my sister felt unreal and strange. I felt like I was living in a nightmare, where my waking life was *just* beyond reach. I tried to write my emotions down, but I often felt too overwhelmed to try to capture my immense sorrow in words. I clung to Danielle's service dog Bruno as a way to hold her, too. I would cry for days, and then be unable to cry at all, wondering if I would ever be able to cry again. I felt panicked because each day that passed meant another day further away from the last time I held or talked to my sister. I started saving everything I had of her. I compiled all of her videos she sent over text. I downloaded programs to save her text messages to me. I would wake in the middle of the night, screaming, and be unable to fall back asleep, scared that any record I had of her would disappear in a computer malfunction.

Everything hard copy of hers I have saved and placed into a fireproof and water-resistant lock-box. It is still not safe enough for me—nothing will ever be—but I can sleep better at night, knowing that I have saved this much and am protecting it as best as I can. I am the big sister; I will forever be her protector.

I also felt compelled to write down my memories of her, but, in that first year, this task seemed too gigantic and strange. How could I write down details and anecdotes about someone who was a part of me? My memories of Danielle were nearly as numerous as my memories of myself. It felt like, in the midst of my endless grief, I would have tasked myself with writing a memoir. I know for many writing immediately after the loss can provide structure, support, or a safe outlet for thoughts, but for me, I wanted to connect to my sister by listening to her favorite music, look at photos of her, and cry.

After a while, though, I began to have spurts of memories associated with places or events. So, instead of trying to chronicle her entire life, I bought a journal, and in this journal I continue to write down specific memories I have of her, whenever they arise. These tiny moments are often hilarious and full of inside jokes. The journal is also safely stored, so when a memory pops up away from the journal (as they nearly always do), I email it to myself with a subject line that links to this special journal, and then I re-write the entries in the journal when I am able to.

The second year of my grief was, in some ways, more challenging than the first year. I was so focused in the first year on getting through all holidays and birthdays and anniversaries without her that I had to survive minute-to-minute and figure out what to do on each day where my parents and I had to figure out how to change our family routine without my sister leading the way. What, for example, was I supposed to do on Father's Day, when my sister often had the good ideas about how to celebrate? How did my mom want to face Mother's Day? (In the end, we went to the graveyard and buried beautiful flowers on my sister's grave together with some of her dear friends who showed up to support her on this day.) How would we celebrate my sister's life on her birthday, when she wasn't there to open presents? (We go to her grave with flowers and the ashes of her service dog, Bruno, who died four years after she did. I play some songs she loved, and recent songs that I think she would have loved. We scatter ginkgo leaves sent to us from loved ones around the world.)

During the second year of grieving, it started to sink in that I would not be waking up from this nightmare. I now had memories of holidays and birthdays without my sister. This sadness felt deeper, heavier, and quieter. It was also a little easier, mentally, to move through the second year, because I had already done so once. I had established some patterns I could keep—and others I could change. My memories of my sister, too, during this second year, began to change and soften a bit. Instead of fixating on the emotional pain she was in before she died, I was able to access more memories of happy times and remember her unlinked to her death. These are some of my favorite memories: Danielle as carefree, silly, her wit the smartest I have ever encountered in my life, and her love for everyone around her.

Over the years I learned about post-traumatic growth, which is a term that refers to how some people, after being faced with a traumatic experience, can change in radical and positive ways. Now, whenever I need to make a difficult decision, I tell myself: Surviving Danielle's death is the hardest thing I have ever done and will ever have to do, and that means I am strong enough to make any other hard decision that crosses my path. By recognizing my own strength and calling upon Danielle for additional support, I now make decisions more decisively and confidently than ever before.

The Clef and the Hummingbird

by Heather Sutherland

At the foot of the Penglais Road hill in the Welsh town of Aberystwyth, there is a small, almost shack-looking, one-storey beige building that is the West Coast Tattoo Parlour. I passed it almost daily during my commute to the lectures and seminars and Union Bar nights-out of my undergraduate-student days. And each time I strolled by, I became increasingly tempted to investigate the place more. A friend of mine had had a large red rose with green splayed-out thorns and leaves printed into her lower back, and I thought it was lovely, graceful. At the age of 19/20ish, though I never voiced the thought, I really wanted my own tattoo, something "little and pretty" was my thinking. Then I heard a rumour story about another friend who'd fainted and fallen off a chair due to the pain whilst having one done—I never found out the truth basis of the tale, but nonetheless even the slightest idea that such a needle response could happen kind of put me off. I moved on to other desires.

Now, however, a little over six years on from my little brother and only sibling, Martin, taking his own life, I have two tattoos.

My first tattoo is my "reminder of him." I chose to have it done to tie in with my brother's birthday, three days after my own in August. I decided on a treble clef design that incorporates a semi-colon, tattooed on the inside of my left wrist—the sign of music to symbolize Martin's love and talents; the semi-colon to signify his struggle and passing, and my nod to Project Semicolon (which focuses on the prevention of suicide through raising awareness and fighting the stigma that exists in talking about suicide). The inking experience was more emotional than I had thought it would be, despite how swiftly and efficiently it was carried out. I asked an already-tattooed friend to accompany me—just because I decided to have it done does not mean I forgot the "friend-fainting-and-falling" story. She held my hand and told me to wiggle my toes to give myself a different bodily area to concentrate on whilst the needle pierced my wrist. I was surprised at how much that tip worked, but it didn't stop me from thinking about my brother. I welled up. And then it was all over, and I fell more in love with the image on my skin than I had expected I would.

My second tattoo is my "reminder to self." The timing chosen for having it done, lunchtime in the middle of an average week, tied this one into daily, continuing life. The experience was a bit more surreal than the first—I went on my own, listened to the artists debate the merits of tinned peaches and carrots immediately prior to the inking, and it hurt much, much more. For this image, I chose an outline of a hummingbird positioned on the front of my right ankle, a very visible location for myself every day (especially in the morning). The image was not a random choice—having lived in Mexico for almost two years I've seen a few of these tiny, most beautiful of birds; my husband and I even visited a local café called El Colibrí (The Hummingbird) every week. But these coincidences aside, it is what the hummingbird means that led me to choose the image. This animal is about overcoming challenges, being mini yet full of strength and courage to handle the troubles and pains it encounters. The feathered-friend also symbolises love and looking for the nectar in life at all times, despite the traumas that present. Even its wings adopt the "eternity" figure-of-eight shape.

It is so easy after losing a sibling to suicide to get stuck. It can feel like you're in some kind of time-warp existence because no matter how many new things you do, experiences you have, that one day that changed everything can repeat in your mind at any moment of its choosing, pulling you backwards and demanding your attention over and over again. There is a want to remember and a want to move forward that live in tandem, that are experienced like the rise and fall of sea waves as "the days/months/years since" accumulate. Bad intersects with the good, and sometimes things can feel so inter-tangled with one another that it is hard to suss out where and who exactly you are, especially on an emotional level.

Karen Leader (2015) writes about tattoos as being "stories on the skin" that can represent "layers of meaning" and be empowering for the person who has them. Far from the derogatory connotations they often have, tattoos can be used to creatively symbolise key events and moments in your life, as a means of helping you tell your story. Dickson et. al. (2015) adds to this by referencing Atkinson's 2003 analysis that tattoos can be a means of self/identity expression, especially where there have been "*role transitions,* changes in life that have important impacts on identity" (p. 108). I relate to that very much, and I also take a lot from Leader's (2016) comment that: "Tattoo narratives ... tell a story from the past, but have a unique presentness to them. They do not record a frozen moment in history, but a continual process of becoming" (p. 190).

For me this is how my images work. Skin holds and shows its natural stories through things like aging-caused wrinkles, spots or scars; my tattoos are the special editions I've added to my library. Their permanency on my skin entirely reflects my relationship with my brother, the very marking nature of "the day the world changed" and the continued learning-to-live-with my loss. I want to remember my brother, his person, and his life; I want to remember, as strange as it sounds, that his death was self-inflicted, as a reminder to talk and raise awareness about suicide (as my tattoos can be really helpful as conversation starters), to do my bit in combatting the stigma that it has, but I also want the loss to *not* take over my whole being and life, wishing to live with and despite it. My tattoos help me do all these things. And at a very basic level, sometimes it is simply useful to have externalities to prompt the self when there is a "rough day" going on—my clef gives me something physical to run my finger over, to trace the linc and remember, something to grant permission to indulge and wallow a little; my hummingbird is something physical to help in giving myself comfort (as well as sometimes a good talking to) in terms of "this is just one bad day; remember all the rest and keep going."

Getting my tattoos was not an impulsive act—they were carefully thought out and reasoned in relation to the events and emotions I have lived, and continue to live, through. I'm ever so glad I have them.

References:

Leader, K. (2015). Stories on the skin: Tattoo culture at a South Florida University. *Arts and Humanities in Higher Education: An International Journal of Theory, Research and Practice*, 14(4), 426-446.

Dickson, L., Dukes, R., Smith, H., & Strapko, N. (2015). To ink or not to ink: The meaning of tattoos among college students. *College Student Journal*, 49(1), 106-120.

Atkinson, M. M. (2014). *Tattooed: The sociogenesis of a body art*. Toronto: University of Toronto Press.

Leader, K. (2016). On the book of my body": Women, power, and "tattoo culture." *Feminist Formations*, *28*(3), 174-195.

Losing Louise

by Shelby Drager

I lost my younger sister Louise on February 13, 2011. She was only 18 years old. At the time, she and I lived in an apartment together in Steamboat Springs, Colorado. We weren't just sisters, but best friends as well. We not only lived together, shared a car, and went to the same school (we even had a few of the same classes), but we also did almost everything together. Louise was beautiful, free-spirited, and such a kind and loving girl. We always had so much fun together. Whether we were snowboarding, or simply hanging out watching a movie in our living room, it was always nice being with her.

When she died, I not only lost my younger sister and best friend, but it felt as if I had lost half of myself. After her death, I never stepped foot in the apartment we shared again. I couldn't bear going in there knowing that, not only was she was gone, but that she had taken her life in the place we called home. My life was in complete shambles. Reality did not feel "real." I did not know how I could live again without my sister. How could I go on when the person I called for everything wouldn't pick up the phone anymore? How could I continue when the person I did almost everything with wasn't there to do things with me anymore? At times, I really did not understand how my life could go on without her. I would have good days and definitely bad days, but the first year after her death was undoubtedly the hardest year of my life.

After Louise died, I moved out of Steamboat immediately. I quit my job, dropped out of school, and moved back to my parents' house. Within two months after her death, I got my second driving offense, and my first serious boyfriend broke up with me. I was completely lost. I was doing just about anything I could to escape reality and numb the pain. I was in a very bad place, and it is only by the grace of God that I am at where I am now. I knew I had to go on and be strong for not only myself but also my family and those I love. I am so glad I kept fighting and got through those days. They may have been the darkest days of my life and tested me to my core, but I gained an immense amount of strength and wisdom during that time.

It has now been seven years since Louise has been gone. Although I will never stop missing her, life has definitely gotten more bearable, and I live my life completely differently than I used to. I try to live the best life I can. I have been sober for a year; I am starting a business, and I am looking to buy a home soon. I want Louise to be proud of her sister, and I want to live a life that the rest of my family is happy with as well. My life will never be the same as it was when Louise was alive, and I will always live with P.T.S.D. and an emptiness in my heart. However, I have my parents, two other sisters, a fiancé, and now a niece and nephew; all of whom I live for every day. If Louise's death has taught me anything, it is to be a better person, be kinder to people, and do my best to make this world a better place. I may not get to see Louise on earth again, but if she were here, I know she would be happy with the life I am living now.

Catching Memories

by Jen

I. Memory stones

When my older brother passed seven years ago, I couldn't imagine doing suicide awareness walks or events. I just couldn't be around that many people. Even the thought of it made me feel too anxious. So, one day on a walk, I wrote a message to my brother on a rock and left it to be gently washed away by water.

I started to ask people if they would like to give me the initials of their loved ones who died by suicide, and I would write their initial on a stone. I would sit quietly. Remember my brother. I thought about the people who gave me initials and sent out peace and comfort for them and their loved one. I would take a photo of the stone and send it to the person who gave me their loved one's initials.

I loved doing it and may get back into it. People would tell me that they loved the photograph of their stone so much that they would frame it and send a me picture of the picture framed on their wall. I tried to pick beautiful places – usually by water. I did a few in the snow as well. It brought me peace.

II. Taking photos of strangers

I wanted to do something positive and upbeat in my brother's memory. But I also wanted it low-key … not screaming … I am doing this in the memory of my dead brother, you know?

When he died, I realized how few pictures we had together. Very few. I also realized that people lose people all the time. So, in his memory, I take pictures of people. When there are older people (you know, the ones that still have a real camera), and they stand one at a time taking a picture of something (usually they are on vacation), I run up and offer to take pictures of all of them. I do this at the beach, on the boardwalk, or in a mall—wherever I see people struggling to get that one person in the picture. Sometimes, someone will say that they aren't photogenic. I tell them that someday it will make someone's day to see a picture of them smiling in a photo … no matter what they look like.

III. Never forgotton

I made the angel/memory stones to give peace and comfort to other survivors of suicide. I would look for a beautiful spot and photograph it, giving the survivor something they could look at in memory of their loved one. These photos were symbols that our loved ones are not forgotten. I also made them in honour of my brother and so that he, too, will never be forgotten.

And I love taking pictures. I think that capturing these random people's memories makes me happy. I don't have many pictures of me and my brother as adults, and I feel like he would be happy to know that I am helping others capture memories. I love hearing stories from the people too, whether they are happy or sad. If we chat long enough, I will occasionally bring up my brother, and often I will hear a story of suicide loss in return. So, sometimes it does get the word out, and hopefully the conversations soften the stigma around suicide.

Most importantly, I do both these things because I like positive actions in my brother's memory.

The Gift of Photographs

by Emily Reitenbach-Molina

Dear Sweet Shannon,

Today we should be celebrating your birthday, but, instead, all we are left with are photos of happier times, as you spend another birthday in heaven. Since our birthdays were so close, we used to always celebrate together. I really miss that. There are days that I wish my birthday could just be another day, but, instead, it seems to be another reminder of you not being here with us. We will go to dinner tonight, but that empty seat is always present. That missing piece of our hearts is replaced with the sounds of broken hearts, still beating.

People often ask me why I take so many photos. June 20th, 2010, I took the last photos of my sweet sister. It was Father's Day. Fifteen days later would be the last time I saw Shannon alive, and three days after that, I would receive the phone call that changed my life forever. My only sibling, and big sister, who was supposed to be by my side to grow old with, and laugh about childhood memories with, would no longer be there with me to relive memories.

Life after a suicide goes on, but believe me when I say, it isn't easy. There are days that you wish you could just wake up and hope this was all just a terrible nightmare. It's so weird to me that the people I know now, post-Shannon, do not know her. They can't hear her sweet laughter. She is only alive in the memories and pictures I share with them.

Memories are one of the best gifts we are left with after the loss of a loved one, but even then, it seems that with each year, her voice grows more silent in my head, and the photos begin to age. 2010 gets further and further away, but the pain never leaves. Never again will I have a recent photo of my sister, only the last ones that I took on that day in June. I am thankful for photos.

I used to take off for your birthday, but I guess it's a sign of healing knowing I can go to work and compartmentalize the sadness I feel within my heart. If for some reason I can't hold back my tears, I have given myself permission to embrace whatever emotions that help me to survive life without you, on your birthday and every day in between. After all, emotions are a physical and symbolic reminder of how deeply we love, not a sign of weakness. In order to heal, we need to feel.

Happy Birthday, sweet sister. Until we meet again, dance with the angels!

I love you and miss you, Shannon … Always and forever.

Love,

Emily

In Loving Memory of Shannon Reitenbach 2/8/74 — 7/8/10

Stronger Than the Struggle

by Mary Costello

There are days that I equate my struggle with being broken or shattered. I'm still learning how to overcome that and to think of myself as healing, or rebuilding, instead.

I have learned that our struggles do not make us weak. They make us strong. They show us paths that we weren't aware we had the option to take. They show us a new way of being. A new way of doing. They show us who is truly there for us, unconditionally, and who we can afford to walk away from. Remember today that you are allowed to take time to take care of yourself. Take a break, even if it's only a minute, to breathe and reset yourself. The only person you owe anything to—is you.

Sometimes, we use our pain, our grief to make a difference in the world. On Sunday, I will walk to support the American Foundation for Suicide Prevention, with the team I formed after my brother's passing. Consider doing a walk. Consider helping us break the stigma that keeps people silent.

There is always hope, although sometimes that hope is hard to hold onto. Don't let go.

Remember: You. Are. Worth. It.

Join us for a day of healing, breaking stigmas, bringing awareness … A day of HOPE. Join us, as we make the choice to #BeTheVoice.

Editor's note: to learn more about the American Foundation for Suicide Prevention's Out of the Darkness walks, visit AFSP.org

Out of the Darkness: Prevention and Advocacy as Healing

by Corbin J. Standley

As I approach the eighth anniversary of my brother's passing, and as I reflect on the last year of my life, I've thought a lot about my chosen profession, my personal identity, and how prevention and advocacy have helped to inform both. My life changed forever when I lost my older brother, David, to suicide on June 30, 2010. He was 21 years old at the time, and I was just about to start my senior year of high school. David was—and still is—a tremendous influence on my life, and in the last year, I've come to better understand that influence.

Education

As David had struggled with mental health conditions for much of his young life, I knew early on that I wanted to study psychology. After taking an introductory course in high school, I pursued my undergraduate degree in psychology and am currently pursuing my doctorate. Undoubtedly, this path was laid out for me because of my loss. My education, research, and future career have all been informed by my loss.

For those of us in research—and in most other fields—we're often discouraged from disclosing certain aspects of our personal lives, including our losses. Our work is meant to come first. This culture has always been counterintuitive to me. A professor and colleague of mine, Dr. Rebecca Campbell (2002), discusses this in her book *Emotionally Involved*: "By emotionally engaging our work, we can gain a closer and potentially insightful perspective." In other words, our emotions and our experience can serve as an invaluable "intellectual resource" in the work that we do.

Over the last year, reading this book and speaking with other colleagues who've experienced loss has been encouraging for me and has forced me to confront the tension between my identity as a researcher and my identity as a survivor of suicide loss. The lines between my personal and professional lives are often blurred. Recently, though, I have found that prevention and grassroots advocacy work reignite my passion for research and illustrate its importance. In short, my personal experience informs my research, which in turn informs my prevention and advocacy.

Prevention and advocacy

After losing my brother to suicide, it took two years for me to find my voice. During that time, I buried myself in schoolwork and extra-curricular activities and didn't talk much about my brother outside of my family. In the fall of 2012, that all changed. My dad told me about an event taking place just south of my hometown, and we signed up for our first American Foundation for Suicide Prevention (AFSP) *Out of the Darkness* Walk in Salt Lake City. At this event, for the first time, I truly felt as though I wasn't alone in my experience. I knew that countless others knew what I was going through, and I felt true comfort for the first time in two years.

Since that walk, I have been involved with the Utah and Michigan Chapters of AFSP, survivors' support groups, and other coalitions and committees across both states. In the last couple years, I've also had the opportunity to use my story both as a researcher and as a suicide loss survivor to advocate for suicide prevention and mental health legislation at the state and national levels. I've been able to share my story with senators and representatives across the country, and I have found these experiences to be inspiring, empowering, and even healing for me.

Healing

In joining these groups and doing this work, I have met the most passionate, dedicated, and loyal group of friends and colleagues I could have asked for. This network of compassionate and caring friends has truly made all the difference in my healing journey. In my move from Utah to Michigan, and in my travels across the country, I have found that I have an extended loss and prevention family everywhere.

In this healing process, I have found prevention and advocacy to be one way of reconciling the tension in my own identity. I realize now that I don't need to choose between my researcher and loss survivor identities, but that these can inform each other. Every day, I wish more than anything that David was still here, and that suicide prevention wasn't an expertise I needed to have. At the same time, though, I have found my passion and my path in life as a result of my loss, and in the process, have found healing.

Reference:

Campbell, R. (2002). *Emotionally involved: The impact of researching rape*. New York, NY: Routledge.

Don’t Force Grief

by Lynne

What would I say to someone
who just lost a loved one to suicide?

Don’t force it.
The hours
days
weeks
months
after the funeral are the worst.
Alone, even with the overflowing support from others,
I felt alone.
Trapped in my own thoughts,
repeatedly going through series of conversations
as if I was looking through a telephone directory.

Why am I not crying
as soon as I open my eyes
filled with thoughts of my brother?
Why do I have the energy to eat breakfast?
Why am I getting dressed for work?
Why am I going to work?
I don’t think I should laugh about it
but it’s funny.
Why do I find it funny?
It’s not funny that my brother died
but it’s funny how clueless we all are.
It’s funny
how numb
your body and your mind can be.
I find it funny that I am in this state.

Don't force it.

If I knew someone
during that first year
who had firsthand experience about it,
I think I'd cry a bucket less.

If someone told me not to force it,
I wouldn't force myself to get back to work after two weeks.
I wouldn't force myself to go through
my planned destination wedding
a month after his death.
I wouldn't force myself to feel better
to look better
to fake better.
Because
it won't pass.
The sadness will remain.
It will linger.

I wouldn't force myself to grieve faster.
Because
in my mind
the sooner I get over this "grieving period"
the better.
It will be less painful.

Don't force it.

The memories that I treasure, confuse me.
  are they real?
Or am I creating new memories in my mind?
My fear of forgetting his face …
his voice …
Unfolds into nightmares …
Into a cycle of dreams,
  Where I continuously fail to save him.

To the person who just lost a loved one to suicide:
A promise of brighter days is a joke.
The road ahead will be rough.
But
do not force yourself to function.
Allow your body to recover. Drink water.
Allow your mind and your heart to get settled.

Life will happen.
You will wake up weaker in some days,
and a little braver in some days, too.
But life will keep you in check.
And forcing yourself to do anything,
feel anything
should be reconsidered.
You are grieving as an individual.
Take care of yourself first,
before taking care of others.

The holidays will feel more like a Halloween party.
Everyone wears a costume,
jokes around,
and eventually someone gets pissed.
This is a norm.
Everyone is aware of each other's words, opinion, and thoughts.
So don't force it.
It's okay to wear a full head-to-toe costume.
It's also okay to just add a mole.
Besides, every day will be a dress rehearsal.
Let the show begin.

III

Beyond the First Decade

Living with Gusto

by Tana Nash

I sat numbly at the kitchen table staring at a blank piece of paper, knowing a deadline loomed. In just a short couple of hours I was to have my sister's obituary written and back to the funeral home. How was this possible? I had only found out less than 24 hours ago that she had died. Suicide. My biggest day nightmare had come true.

That was twelve years ago. Although I miss my sister Erin every day and in particular during life milestones with my family, it is no longer that gut-wrenching pain that I experienced following her death. How did I get here? What has helped?

Although each of our journeys is different, and no two sibling relationships are the same, here are some tips that I have found helpful along my healing journey.

First and foremost, I want to reach through the pages and give you a hug and tell you that sibling loss is just as important and difficult. I found it difficult to be "strong for your parents" as I was repeatedly told by well-wishers who didn't understand how painful that was to hear. I had lost a sister! Who was going to be strong for me? What I would have loved to know is there are other sibling loss survivors who understand the pain.

Reading for me was instrumental. The two most helpful books I found were *Night Falls Fast: Understanding Suicide* (2000) by Kay Redfield Jamison and *No Time to Say Goodbye: Surviving the Suicide of a Loved One* (1999) by Carla Fine. I journaled and scribbled my love and thoughts. Boxing proved to be a great outlet as I punched my deep sadness onto the heavy bag. Individual counseling and a suicide-specific grief group were instrumental in helping me move through my grief.

I learned key mantras that I still use today: "Don't SHOULD on yourself and don't let others SHOULD on you either." I repeat this powerful mantra when my mind tries to guilt me: "I should have done this" "I could have done that." The "would have," "should have" and "could have" phrases will eat you up inside if you let them.

I learned to be gentle to myself and to be kind in my thoughts and to my body. Grief takes a tremendous amount of work. I learned how grief manifests itself in four key ways: emotional, physical, spiritual, and behavioral. Just as I was encouraged, take a blank piece of paper and draw a quadrant. In each quadrant, write one of the four words and describe how grief is rearing its head for you. When I completed this exercise, I wasn't sure at first which one to include. But once I started writing, I was surprised to see each of my quadrants filling up. For example, in the emotional square, I wrote that I was irritable and testy, and crying unpredictably. For physical, I found that more grey hairs were coming in, that my back and shoulders were full of knots and that my eczema was worse. Grief was actually manifesting itself in my body and showing me how and where! In the spiritual quadrant, I wrote that I was questioning the meaning of life and what do I do next. What's really important now? And finally, in the behavioral quandrant, I found that I was no longer reading the paper every day—an activity I previously enjoyed. I just simply didn't have the energy. Using these examples as a base for yourself, begin to fill in the four quadrants.

You might be surprised to see how full your page is. Now repeat to yourself, saying your own name first: "Be gentle and be kind."

I also learned to differentiate between who was giving me energy and who was taking it away. This was no time to be surrounded by energy sucking vampires. I gave myself time to heal and permission to love and laugh.

With time and work can come something beautiful: something I have learned is called post-traumatic growth. Post-traumatic growth is the ability to not only heal following a tragedy but to actually use the crisis as a catalyst to further learn and grow. This growth has brought me new perspectives and a new lens with which to view my loss that is much healthier. Doing the work is really important. Most likely, like me, you are not equipped to deal with this loss and need new strategies, new tools in the toolbox. It isn't easy, but it is possible. This loss will always be stitched into your heart. Be grateful for the sibling you had and the incredible memories you shared. Embrace them, celebrate them, and take them with you as you go on. I encourage you to live with gusto in honor of the sibling you hold in your heart.

References:

Fine, C. (2000). *No time to say goodbye: Surviving the suicide of a loved one*. New York, NY: Broadway Books.

Jamison, K. R. (2012). *Night falls fast: Understanding suicide*. London: Picador.

Johnny's Little Sister

by WyKisha Thomas-McKinney

It had been more than twelve years since I had seen them: friends from Johnny's inner circle. When Johnny and I first moved to Houston in 2000, they were our family, complete with Sunday dinners, group outings, and adopted uncles for my son. When he died, they were all there, helping to plan the funeral and shield my parents and me from any negativity or drama that transpired. After he died, they all slowly faded away. Over the years, I had spoken to one or two of them sporadically, sharing dialogue, liking pictures and status updates on Facebook. For many of them, though, it was too hard for them to see me. It brought back memories of what used to be and reopened old wounds. I understood that … It hurt … But I understood.

J., the patriarch of our makeshift family, invited me to attend a forum on mental illness and suicide in the LGBT community. I first met J. when he accompanied my brother on a visit to my dorms. J. and Johnny worked together in the LGBT community helping to prevent new HIV infections. From the moment we met, J. embraced me as family. His love and concern for my brother and me would be invaluable in the days following Johnny's suicide.

I was excited but also nervous to attend the forum. Would someone break down crying when they saw me? Would I break down crying? Do they even remember who I am? Who Johnny is? Will my depression be triggered? Despite the questions swirling in my head, I couldn't wait to see J. and possibly some of our other old friends, again. I think I felt that by being with them that I would feel closer to my brother. Anxiety swelled in my chest as I entered the room. Meanwhile, people shuffled about from one group to the other: talking, laughing, exchanging business cards … Doing what people do at these types of events. I scanned the room for familiar faces but saw none. My chest tightened even more. But then I heard a familiar sound come from the other side of the room: J.'s infectious laugh. Our eyes set on each other, and he rushed over and gave me the warmest embrace. My anxiety immediately melted.

J. wrapped his arm around me and began introducing me to his colleagues. "Hey, remember Johnny? This is his little sister," he would say as he moved me from one person to the other. "You know Johnny's little sister, the one I was telling you about … Does all the work for suicide prevention." We maneuvered again, "Meet Johnny's little sister." And again, "Remember the baby I used to keep with me all the time? This is his mom. Yeah, Johnny's little sister."

Nostalgia swept over me as "Johnny's little sister" rang in my ear over and over again. No one had referred to me as "Johnny's little sister" since before he died. In fact, I distinctly remember asking myself, "Who am I, now that he's gone?" I asked that very question at his funeral. I remember specifically saying to someone, "I don't know who I am anymore if I'm not his sister." When you've spent your entire life being something to someone else and then they're gone, what does that leave you with? So that's where the struggle is, I think, for people who lose their sibling. We fight to find peace with our new role, our new normal, without forgetting that we were (are) someone's sister or brother.

I never realized how strong a bond could be between siblings until I felt the absence of the bond between my brother and me. My mother loves to tell stories of how Johnny had morning sickness and sympathy pains when I was pregnant and in labor with my son and how I could always sense when Johnny was about to get sick (he was HIV positive). As kids, Johnny and I fought like cats and dogs. We would pick at each other all the time, play terrible tricks, and do things to get the other person in trouble. On the other hand, it was us against the world; if there was a problem with one of us, there was a problem with both of us. I have four half-siblings as well, but Johnny is who I grew up with and was closest to. We would literally go to war for each other. When I became pregnant, at 19, with my son, my brother prepped my parents for the discussion by demanding that they approach the conversation with a positive attitude or there would be hell to pay. As his older sister, I was always protective of Johnny and let people know I would not stand for anyone being insensitive about my brother's sexuality. What stands out most for me, though, is that we had major plans. Plans that all went away when he took his life. We had everything laid out:

Plan A: We would stack our money and buy a house together. Nothing extravagant; just something affordable and manageable in case we had to live on one income. This way I could be there to take care of him when he got sick, and we wouldn't have to worry about paying rent for two places.

Plan B: If/When the time came to where he was too sick to care for himself, I would quit my job, and we would move back to Dallas with our parents. This way I could take care of him and have help with my son.

He didn't stick to the plan—OUR PLAN! And suicide was certainly never a part of our plans! I was so angry with him for that. Then, I was angry with myself for getting angry with him. It was only after I gave myself permission to be upset with him that I began to heal from losing him. I had gone to counseling, tried support groups, medications, you name it. And all of those things were helpful to an extent. However, the one thing that I couldn't seem to bring myself to do, and that I needed to do, was be angry with Johnny. I would justify this by saying, "How can I be mad at him? He was sick," or, "This isn't about me. He didn't do this to hurt me." Then one day, maybe about six or seven years after his death, I just got so frustrated with him. I thought about all the things in my life and my children's lives that he's missed. I thought about all the things I could have really used his help on. I thought about taking care of our parents on my own. I thought about how he left me here, alone. Most of all, I thought about all our plans that would never be. Then I got mad! I mean really pissed! And I accepted that anger. The way I see it, it's just like when we were kids. Johnny always did things to annoy me and I would get mad at him all the time, but that didn't mean I loved him any less. So, being angry with him now has no bearing on how much I love him. I love my brother more than anything … He just really burns me up sometimes (I say this with a smile on my face).

It has now been 14 years since Johnny died, and boy, has it been a struggle. Surviving suicide loss is definitely a wild journey with many turns, detours, and setbacks. Nonetheless, what I can promise to all the siblings out there who are trying to figure out "what now?" is this: First, you're still their sibling. Nothing, not even death, can change that. Second, your sibling's death was just a change in the plans. Frustrating? Yes, of course. No one likes last-minute changes in their plans, but with time you will adjust and thrive. Next, you will survive this. Now, as cliché as that sounds, I really mean it. I know you might be thinking, "Yeah, right. I have some beachfront property in Idaho for sale, too." It's true, though! Over time, you'll find that it's just a little bit easier to get up in the morning, and the memories don't hurt as bad. Just keep getting up; it will get easier. Finally, while you may not have your blood sister or brother with you anymore, you have a multitude of brothers and sisters in the cause. Embrace this new family and let us help you heal. While Johnny and my plans have changed, one thing that has certainly remained the same … I am still and forever will be Johnny's little sister.

Finding a Way through the Darkness: Becoming a Sister on a Mission

by Sally Spencer-Thomas

People remember in vivid detail where they were when John F. Kennedy was shot or when the World Trade Centers were hit. It's called a "flashbulb" memory—the moment is forever engraved in your psyche as if a picture had been taken. The moment my mom told me my brother had killed himself, I was in my car with my three sons, who were six years old, three years old, and three months old. It was December 7, 2004.

The kids and I were on our way to a holiday party hosted by my students at one of their homes. As usual, I was a bit harried and running late, but our moods were cheerful. A wrapped Yankee Swap present bounced around somewhere in the back of my Toyota RAV4. The scent of cloves wafted through the vehicle from the ham I was bringing for the dinner. A poinsettia was balanced precariously on the front seat. My children were practicing "I Have A Little Dreidel." I was wearing a god-awful '80s red-and-white Christmas sweater with snowman earrings—and smiling to myself about how much I had become my mother. It was a light moment after a stressful fall. My brother had been very ill with depression, and I had been on maternity leave following the birth of my third son. I was looking forward to reconnecting with my students and celebrating the passage of another year. My heart was filled with optimism.

I was probably speeding a little along I-76 on that cold evening as I tried to make up time, knowing I had the main dish to deliver and that dozens of hungry students were waiting for our arrival. It was dark, and I was driving from my home in the foothills of the Rocky Mountains to Broomfield, a Denver suburb, about an hour away.

My cell phone rang. I fumbled for it in my purse and told the kids to stop singing. I normally would not answer the phone while driving with them in the car, but my brother had been in crisis, so …

"Where are you? Do you have the boys with you?" Mom asked. I told her I had all three of them, and I happened to be nearing the Federal Boulevard exit—the one I would take to get to my parents' house had I been headed there. The exit to get to the party was still a long way off.

"Pull over," she commanded.

My stomach immediately tensed, and I felt queasy. *Don't jump to conclusions*, I reminded myself. *You are always labeled as the dramatic one; keep your cool.* Where was that exit?

"Hold on, Mom. I am trying to get to the exit. Hold on." Silence. *Why is she not saying anything? Where is the exit?*

Finally, I'm able to merge to the right and slide onto the gravel shoulder. "Okay, Mom, what is it?" I really don't want to know.

"Sally, put the car in park." Her voice sounds serious, but she is not crying. Maybe it is not so bad.

"Mom, you are killing me. What is it?" *I don't want to know; I don't want to know.* There is a bowling ball of tar sinking in my gut and collapsing my lungs.

"Our worst fears are confirmed. Carson has killed himself."

I drop the phone and scream. The sound comes from deep inside—an awful, inhuman scream. I open the car door and yell and curse, while my racing thoughts try to process what she said: *Did she say "killed?" Surely, she meant attempt to ... Or maybe he is just missing, and she is jumping to conclusions. She didn't mean killed ... That can't be possible. Not Carson, not Carson, not Carson ...*

I am totally out of my mind. Where is the air? More screaming. I don't know where I am. I don't know what I am doing. What happened to the phone? I must find the phone. I dig around on the floor of my car, focused on this singular mission. I feel like I am out of my body.

Then a small voice from the back seat brings me back to reality. It's my six-year-old. At the very sweet age of six, he knows his Uncle Carson as a magical person, someone who flips kids over his shoulder and makes up silly rhymes with my son's name in them. Someone who was teaching him how to ski and the finer points of bowling between the legs and shooting pool. Someone who had danced around the room with my son in his arms, rocking out to Barenaked Ladies. In a tender voice, my six-year-old son asks, "Did something happen to Uncle Carson?" And then, after a moment or two with no coherent response, he says, "Mommy, I am crying for you."

I am on the side of the dark and icy highway on my hands and knees looking for my phone. Although I felt like a piece of glass that had been shattered into a thousand pieces on the road, that tiny voice sliced through the chaos and brought me back. I know it sounds crazy, but in that instant, I knew that I couldn't stay shattered there on the road; I had to find a way to pull the pieces back together, for the boys in the backseat, for my mother on the other end of that phone. I finally found the phone and focused. The next step was remembering how to drive. I remember pulling every internal resource I had to bear on the task of driving the 50 blocks up Federal Boulevard to reach my parents' house. Maybe when I got there, we could figure this out. I remember concentrating on the lights—red means stop, green means go—and counting down the blocks left to go until we were safe.

Later that night, my father returned home, ashen and stoic. The family had all gathered at my parents' house, and we started to put the puzzle of that day together. Carson woke up at my parents' house that morning and had put on one of his best business suits. He had told my father that he was going out to meet with his business associates and let them know that he was going to take some time off from work to tend to his health and his wife and daughter. Carson said all the right things. He was calm. My father never saw him alive again.

Carson stopped at his former office in downtown Denver to return a shirt. His co-workers later noted that he seemed anxious, but they didn't make much of it at the time. From there he went to his industrial-style loft and died, alone and in despair. As the hours passed and no one heard from him, frantic calls started to fly back and forth between my family members. Has anyone heard from Carson? No. Finally, around 4 p.m., my father took the key my brother had given him, made the dreaded trip to the loft, and discovered his son's body. Hours later, the first responders had completed their investigation for the night, and my father came home. He then stated he was going to bed.

Six months earlier

In May 2004, my brother had his first full-blown episode of bipolar disorder. He had been diagnosed in college but managed his illness in its milder form through a combination of medication, on-and-off therapy, and substance abuse; only the immediate family knew. Carson was a highly successful entrepreneur, an accomplished athlete, and a friend to many. He was the mentor people sought out when they had a problem. He was a creative visionary, a compassionate friend when people needed a listening ear, and an enthusiastic supporter of all who were embarking on big adventures. And he was pee-in-your-pants funny. But the summer of 2004 was different. For reasons we didn't—and still don't—fully understand, his disorder took a drastic turn for the worse. Maybe it was because he quit taking his Paxil cold turkey or because he'd stopped drinking, but for whatever reason, he catapulted into mania: He left his wife and daughter, left his business partner, and bought a $1 million loft downtown, an $80,000 car, and laptops for employees he didn't have. He said he was trying to launch a national insurance company and even had ideas for a world hockey league.

He was agitated and mean. I wanted so desperately for

him to connect with me, but after every phone call with him I found myself in tears. After one such exasperating conversation, I handed the phone to my husband, who told Carson that he was making me too upset, and my brother threatened legal action against me. One by one, he lashed out at all the family members, believing we had all turned on him.

Carson didn't sleep for days. In October, he spontaneously got on a plane to Chicago and didn't bring a coat. When Thanksgiving came, he had spent his last penny and couldn't get any more because his credit cards had reached their limits. He crashed into a depression so debilitating he was unrecognizable. The family rushed in—we had love, resources, and knowledge—yet he still died.

I remember sitting with him the week before his death. He was in what I now know to be an agitated-depressive state, the worst of both mania and depression. He wore a wool coat all night as he paced around my parents' home and tried to find warmth next to their gas fireplace. He had lost 30 pounds in a month. His hands shook, making it difficult for him to write, and he chain-smoked and consumed caffeinated beverages constantly. On that last night I saw him alive, we sat on my parents' white couch in the formal living room; between us was a copy of Dr. Kay Redfield Jamison's *An Unquiet Mind.* Her brave memoir chronicles her life as a professor of psychiatry at Johns Hopkins Medical School, her near fatal suicide attempt, and her battles with bipolar disorder. The book describes the challenges of getting treatment and how she eventually learned to manage her illness.

Our copy of the book was well worn by the time I sat down with Carson that night. The whole family had taken turns reading it when Carson was at the height of his mania. We had all felt so helpless like we were watching a train wreck but couldn't do anything to stop it. One of the cruelest things about bipolar disorder is that when people are in the throes of it, they are absolutely convinced they are right. During the summer, Carson believed that all the decisions he was making were ones he should have made a long time ago, and that his close friends and family had turned against him because we were questioning his judgment. When he became depressed, he came back to us, so I was grateful that I had that time on the couch with him, talking about Dr. Jamison's book. I asked if he wanted to read it. He shook his head and asked me what it was about. I told him about her story. "See? Another hugely successful person, just like you. She struggled and she got better." There is hope, there is hope, there is hope.

He turned to me and whispered, "But Sally … It's madness."

Less than a week later, he was dead.

I have replayed that evening a million times over in my head. In hindsight, I believe Carson was trying to tell me that even if he made it through this unbelievable psychological torment he was experiencing, he questioned who would be there for him on the other side.

Tsunami

Carson died on December 7, the anniversary of the bombing of Pearl Harbor, two weeks before Christmas, and two weeks before his 35th birthday. It was also two weeks before the Asian tsunami hit. As the world reacted to that disaster, the aftermath of Carson's death similarly hit our family; we, too, were flooded with feelings of helplessness, of being overwhelmed. The news of his suicide crashed tsunami-like around us, totally engulfing us in despair and darkness. Frozen and in shock, we fought for every breath, thinking, *This cannot be happening*. I confused night with day, day with night. I remember feeling very vulnerable. I would be driving to the airport to pick up a guest for Carson's memorial service, and I would look up and have no idea where I was or what I was doing. Then I would be hit by a wave of panic as I was sure everyone on the road was going to hit my car.

After the memorial service, after the holidays, after my maternity and bereavement leave was up, I needed to resurface. I remember coming up for air and looking around: The landscape had changed because my brother was no longer in it. Everything looked and felt different. Things that were so desperately important before no longer mattered. Just like the tsunami, the ripple effects of his death spread deep and wide, and to this day still continue to impact those who knew him. Thanks to social media, I still periodically connect with people Carson knew who are just now learning of his passing.

The aftershocks of the trauma were severe at first, some of them predictable, like on Father's Day, his death anniversary, and his birthday. Others caught us off guard like the time I was digging through a box of photos. I was searching for pictures of us together so I could make a collage. I found one of me holding him as a baby under the Christmas tree. He was born on Christmas Eve, so I always said he was my favorite Christmas gift. There was the one of us dancing as little children in coordinating velvet formal wear my mother had made. There was the picture of us mugging for the camera with our eyes crossed and goofy grins as my mother, off-camera, begged us to smile nicely. There was a picture of us relaxing on the dock overlooking the harbor at Martha's Vineyard, and a black-and-white one of us cheek-to-cheek from high school. I looked at each of them and thought, *And he loved me, he loved me, he loved me*. And then I found a picture I had forgotten about, of us dancing at my wedding. Not many brothers and sisters dance to their own song when they get married to another person, but Carson and I had a song: Whitney Houston's "I Will Always Love You." Whenever we heard it on the radio, we would belt it out to each other at the top of our lungs, being as silly as possible. At my wedding, Carson and I twirled around the dance floor—my hair coming loose from my updo, his shirt hanging untucked from his tuxedo. Someone snapped a picture as we joyously sang the chorus, eyes locked and laughing. When I found this picture, I wept and wept. Then I made a copy of it to hang next to my computer so I would never forget.

As with the tsunami, the rebuilding process has been long and hard, requiring many systems of support. In this sense I often feel lucky, because unlike many survivors of suicide I had a workplace that was supportive, a faith community that understood his suicide as the fatal outcome of a mental illness (not a crime against God), and a network of friends who did all the right things.

On the day my brother died, I had been a psychologist for nine years, four months, and three days, and in the field of mental health for much longer than that. I knew about suicide. I had studied it. I had even published a research paper with my mentor for the FBI Academy on police officers' response to civilian suicide just five years earlier. And I was completely humbled by the life-changing impact of Carson's death. I realized that I knew about suicide and mental illness in my head, but I did not appreciate the full human implications in my heart.

Upon reflection, three things stand out to me about the shifts I have experienced since Carson died. First, I have a profound respect for the power of mental illnesses in a way I could not fathom before. Bipolar disorder was like a thief in the night, stripping my brother of his spirit and stealing his soul. The brain is a master organ, and when it went awry, it took complete control over Carson's physical, relational, financial, and, of course, emotional well-being, all in the blink of an eye.

Second, I have come to appreciate the complex nature of suicide bereavement. While I had experienced loss before, this was different. My grandparents had lived into their seventies and eighties and died of chronic illnesses over time; my pets had also lived long and healthy lives.

When Carson died, I was completely overwhelmed with the intensity and complexity of the feelings stirred inside me. On one level, I was dealing with grief in its rawest form. Suicide often takes people who are otherwise perfectly healthy physically and should have lived another several decades. When you consider all the life lost, all the potential, all the scripts of how things were going to be, the hole that's created is very deep. The grief is compounded by the abrupt and traumatic nature of suicide.

The horror of self-inflicted violence cannot be underestimated, and while I was spared the death scene, I was still haunted by its image in my mind and played out my interpretation of my brother's final moments again and again. Finally, even if you can find your way through the grief and trauma, there is always an ache that resides just below the breastbone, reverberating with the never-answered question, "Why?"

The third thing I learned is that mental health is not an "us" (who are healthy) and "them" (who are ill) issue, as I had believed as one who studied these issues and as a clinician. It is a "we" issue. We are all touched by mental health conditions at some point in our lives. About 20% of us will experience the death of a family member to suicide, and around 60% will know someone who died by suicide over the course of our lives. We don't appreciate how common the life and death struggle is because of the secrecy that shrouds suicidal behavior. Many of the mental health conditions are spectrum disorders, meaning that they have both milder and more severe forms, and people can move up and down those spectrums for various reasons. I developed a deep respect for the people I meet who fought the demons of depression and other mental health conditions or who survived a suicide attempt and who have persisted in their recovery. We have so much to learn about the resiliency of these heroes because their stories of success are not shared enough.

"Heroes" is not a word often used in conjunction with suicide attempt survivors, but to me, that is what they are. Most have experienced unimaginable psychological pain and have had to fight their way back to life, usually while being horribly misunderstood and often completely on their own. Just as we think of cancer survivors as heroes in their fight for life, so I think of those who have conquered life-threatening mental illnesses.

I don't share my story because I want pity or because I need empathy. While losing Carson has been the most difficult experience of my life, I have also received many gifts along my grief journey. I was reminded of this by the leader of the rock group Seether who lost his younger brother to suicide and wrote a song called "Rise Above This" on the album *Finding Beauty in Negative Spaces.* This too has been my experience in grief: rising above. I have found new depth in relationships and in my spirituality, as well as an unwavering calling of vocation. I tell this story because so few families do, and the consequence is that people think it can never happen to them. While I am humbled by my experience, I am also hopeful. Suicide is arguably one of the more preventable causes of death, so I also share this story in hopes that others will come forward and say, "I, too, have been affected, and I want to make a difference. How can I get involved?" And finally, I share this story because people who are in a suicidal crisis often think that those who love them will be better off without them. I am here to tell them that suicide causes a legacy of trauma and pain that continues for generations. No matter how hard it gets, you never know what is waiting for you around the corner.

Upward and outward: Advocacy for resilience, mental health, and suicide prevention

The journey into mental health advocacy often starts in a personal way. Somehow, someway, your life has been touched by mental illness or suicide, and you can see how things could be different.

The night that Carson died, his good friend from Atlanta called my sister-in-law and asked, "What can I do?"

She replied, "Whatever you do, don't let him be forgotten."

That became my mission too. The night of my brother's death the seeds were planted to start an effort to do bold, gap-filling work to prevent what happened to Carson from happening to other people, and to lift up his legacy of helping others.

Through partnerships with dozens of local, national, and international organizations, I have learned there is much to be hopeful about. What I have learned since I joined the mental health promotion and suicide prevention movement is that there is a role for everyone in this life-saving work—and there is so much work to be done. I have also been inspired by the many people who have lived through their own suicidal intensity and suicide grief who are pulling together to make our world safer from suicide. I hope wherever you are in your grief journey, you consider joining us someday.

One of my many role models is Helen Keller. After losing her sight and hearing at 19 months old, Helen went on to conquer seemingly insurmountable challenges in communication and activism. To me, she is a role model for mental resiliency. She made a lifelong effort to remap the boundaries of what is possible, while dedicating herself to radical social justice with a keen sense of optimism.

I want to do the same. My daily mantra is a quote by E. B. White: "I get up every morning determined to both change the world and have one hell of a good time. Sometimes this makes planning my day difficult."

Didi's Legacy

by Vanessa McGann

I lost my sister to suicide over 15 years ago. I had so many feelings in the beginning: shock, terror, deep sadness, shame, and even a bit of relief (for the end of her pain and the end of my worry). But paramount among those feelings was fear—fear about one specific thing: how her suicide would impact my children. To be honest, there was a bit of anger mixed in with that fear, too. After all, she was my sister; at times she had been competitive, she had been mean, and she had been thoughtless in a sisterly way. But she had never been cruel. Killing herself when I had young children felt utterly cruel to me.

It made sense to me that, after years of battling intense depression, my sister might decide to end her life. But it didn't make sense that she might put my children at risk. At the time of her death, my children were one and three. How could she put such a shadow over the early years of their development? How would my baby take in my sorrow, my weight loss, my tears, and my trauma? How would my toddler understand the death of her Aunt Didi and understand the loss of that special connection they had already formed? And how would they both feel when they were teenagers, if they became depressed, and if (and when) they suffered their own traumas? I felt terrified that my sister's act would allow them to feel that suicide was an option. I felt terrified that her death would damage them.

I asked my therapist how to tell my three-year-old daughter. He suggested I say that Didi had an accident. That didn't seem right. I asked someone else who suggested that I say that she was very sick and died. That didn't seem right either. As it turned out, I didn't really have to say much at the time. I simply told her

"Mommy has been so much crying because Aunt Didi died." She looked up at me and asked: "Are you going to die?" I said no. "Is Daddy going to die?" I said no. Then my beautiful daughter went off and did what she needed to do: she played.

It wasn't that my grief and my sister's death didn't affect my daughter early on. She had trouble separating from me in her nursery school. She engaged in some rigid play about being a baby bird that needed help to eat, walk, and fly. It was sweet doing this play with her; it was even a bit healing for me, but it could go on repetitively and had a slightly desperate feel showing how she needed to be nurtured and protected. I also remember being upset with myself (and my sister) as I would often get simple things mixed up a lot in those early days—so I would bring my daughter to a birthday party on the wrong day or to a play date at the wrong location. And I felt very isolated around other new mothers. I think they did not want to spend time with me in my grief, and I found it hard to engage in their friendly but superficial chitchat and common motherly worries.

One of my worst moments was during a winter celebration at my daughter's nursery school. Though crowded with parents, no one was sitting next to me. And as the toddlers all stood in rows wearing silver wreaths on their adorable heads, my daughter looked pale and scared and did not participate in the joyous holiday singing. I remember sobbing in the bathroom, wondering if my daughter would have been as shy and frightened had my sister been alive and had I been stronger, and knowing I would never be able to know the answer.

Time went on, and we found our way. There were a few funny but somewhat morbid stories. Like the time my brother and I put my sister's ashes in the ocean without showing them to my daughter. She got so sad and angry that I felt the need to take some ashes from our outdoor grill and tell her that they were Nadine. And apparently, when my daughter was six, she wanted her little brother to get out of the bathtub. So, in typical sister fashion, she told him that my sister had died because she stayed too long in the bathtub. My terrified three-year-old son ran to me and asked if I had a sister and if so, was she dead. I of course said yes, and he of course developed a fear of bathing until my daughter eventually confessed and we straightened things out. There were also some initial hints that Nadine's death might not lead to their fear or fragility. I remember my son's second grade class was instructed to write condolence letters to a devastated community who lost many members to an earthquake. While many children wrote things like: "try to be happy" or "I am so sorry" he wrote: "look into your heart and you will still see your family there."

I never hid my sister's suicide from my kids. When they asked questions about her, I would answer as best I could for their age level and understanding. I don't think they would say that was a moment when they "found out" that she took her life; they always knew because I talked about her often, and I did not withhold the fact of her suicide. And when they asked how she killed herself, I told them. And when they asked why she killed herself, I tried my best to explain. Sometimes we even joke together, not in a mean way about Nadine or her death, but about suicide in general. I feel good about this—I feel that using humor is a way of exploring and managing difficult ideas and emotions.

My kids are now teens. They have of course hit rough patches, but they are strong and resilient. I will not deny that I can still have a quick moment when I fear I might one day lose them, but I am not at all terrified in the way I used to be. In an unexpected fashion, I feel they are quite grounded and have grace, warmth, wisdom, and an ability to reach out to others in a very special way.

Fifteen years later, I finally ran out of all the wrapping paper I inherited from my sister, so I no longer get to give presents to my kids with a trace of my sister's decor enveloping them. And all of the little punk T-shirts, purple glitter jeans and obnoxiously loud plastic toys she gave them to drive me crazy are all in storage, donated, or discarded. I wish I still had her here to give my kids presents that, especially in comparison to me, she was always so good at picking out; I wish I had her here to tell my kids stories about our parents, to edit their papers, and to share with them her biting and sarcastic wit.

There are two aspects of my sister's death and its impact on my kids that I did not consider in those early days. First, they know about suicide. It is not taboo to talk about in my house, nor is it fetishized in any way. For that reason, I think that it will never feel like an option for them in the direct way I feared when she first died. Maybe it will be even less of an option for them than it would have been had she still been alive. Second, they know their Aunt Nadine. They know she was political; they know she was a feminist. They know she was super smart and that she was a great writer and photographer. They know she loved dogs and rescued and trained them. They know she was my sister whom I loved and who loved me in return. In other words, they know who their aunt was as a beautiful complex sister first and as a person who died by suicide second.

In many ways, and I know this is cliché, her death has given me unforeseen gifts. I feel more passionate in loving my children, I feel more in touch with the poignant moments of growth and change, and I feel more able to confront the fears, sorrows, and accomplishments of myself and my loved ones. My anger at Nadine has vanished, and in its place is understanding, acceptance, and love.

Still a Good Life

by Michelle L. Rusk

Whether I liked it or not, my younger sister Denise knew more about me—and what I wanted out of life—than anyone else.

After her suicide death in 1993, I struggled for a long time with the thought that she took half our childhood memories with her (although some days I remind myself there are things it's probably better she can't tell my husband about me!) when she died.

However, as life has gone forward, my perspective of much of around her death has changed. And I have come to realize that she and our parents—who died after her—are my biggest cheerleaders. They might not be here on earth with me, but the signs are all around me that they are here. That continuing bond never broke. Instead, it changed, and it was up to me to integrate it into my life although in a different way than I had been accustomed to.

My life has taken many twists and turns since I was a 21-year-old, faced with the unthinkable: the suicide of my sister. I was forced to mature and grow in ways that no one my age could truly understand. They tried as best they could, but my life was forced into a trajectory that I couldn't control.

What I could control was what I chose to do with it and ultimately the road led me to writing *Do They Have Bad Days in Heaven? Surviving the Suicide Loss of a Sibling*. That book—one of the first for the sibling suicide bereaved—took me around the world speaking, helped me earn a doctorate in family studies, to writing more books, and finally to the American Association of Suicidology presidency.

I have done amazing things; I have met amazing people. But at some point on the road, I realized that if I kept doing all this work, I would not be the person I'm supposed to be. There are a lot of things I *can* do in my life; however, it doesn't mean they are the things I'm *supposed* to do. This became clearer after my dad died in 2006 and then my mom in 2014. Their deaths also pushed Denise's death further into my past. It doesn't mean her death means less. I've had a lot more time to digest it, move forward, and weave her into my life in a different way than them. And I spoke and wrote about her death so much that I long ago let go of fact that it was a suicide and instead remember her for the nearly eighteen years we had with her, rather than how she ended it.

Since I was six years old, I wanted to be a writer—not of self-help books like eight of the ten I have written—but of fiction. I wanted to tell stories, especially those of the characters that reside in my head. And it was not long after I finished my doctorate that I realized I needed to return to that road.

Back in 1999 I had been querying both fiction and the sibling book to publishers (it was different in those days—you could contact an editor directly rather than the route now of finding an agent first). But the opportunity came first to publish the sibling suicide work, and so the fiction novel I'd written got pushed aside, usually to a pile on the floor next to my desk.

Things took off with the suicide work, and while I didn't think I would be working in the suicidology field forever, it was where I was at, there was much to do, and I was quite content to be part of it.

Then one day I pictured Denise saying to me, "I appreciate all you've done for sibling survivors but don't forget who you were before I died. Don't forget the goals and dreams that you had."

I hadn't forgotten any of it. I had just put away like the stuff we shove in the closet that we believe we might need one day, that we don't want to throw out or give away.

I then made a concerted effort to return to my fiction, and today there is a second aspect to that creative route: Chelle Summer.

Denise and I learned to sew together. I remember all the time we spent in our parents' bedroom where Mom had set up her sewing area. Mom taught us using her mother's old Singer machine (the kind with a cabinet plus a bench to sit on). We made endless amounts of clothes for our Barbie dolls.

Mom encouraged our creativity; there was always paper to draw on, and we always seemed to receive crayons and markers for Christmas. She took us to the fabric store with her, and we were allowed to pick out a remnant each so we could make our Barbie clothes.

Sewing and creating had been important to me for a long time. A neighbor I had considered my second mom and who died three weeks before my dad passed away taught me how to quilt and do some other creative endeavors—but, as the suicide work picked up and I entered my doctoral work, I had put it all aside.

And yet, one day it returned. There are several events that led to it, none at least obviously related to my sister, but all to my life today. I had just been married again, and we were in the Old Navy store at the outlet mall in Barstow, California, when I was griping about how they had these cool colored denim shorts but they never made them as miniskirts.

"Why don't you make them then?" Greg asked me.

It took me a moment, and I realized, why not?

The other piece involved a bucket bag from the back of *Vogue* magazine that inspired me. I had an idea of something similar I wanted to make.

As I started to spend more time creating, the ideas flowing quickly (probably too quickly in many ways!), I sensed that *this* is who I'm supposed to be. It's a balance of telling stories through writing but also through creating handbags, clothes, and other items that reflect my style. It's all giving me a way to share all that my parents and my sister helped me cultivate as I grew as a person.

It just took me a while to get here because I had a road I had to travel before I could arrive at this one. And it's a road that my sister, and my parents, go forward with me.

Three Brothers, Two Suicides, One Survivor

by Dennis Gillan

Phone rings, life changes. Happens to the best of us. It was after work on Monday, July 18, 1994 when the phone rang in my home in Carlisle, PA. I was home waiting for my wife to come home from work when I got the word that my little brother Matthew was gone. In a drunken stupor with access to lethal means, gone. I remember sitting on the couch, waiting for my wife, and thinking to myself that we already did this; we already did this. You see, eleven years earlier, I received a similar phone call telling me that my older brother Mark lost his battle to depression.

Let me decode the last paragraph for you: my name is Dennis Gillan, and I have lost two brothers to suicide. It hurts to type it, and for years I could not even say the word suicide without crying. Now I am a mental health advocate and speak about suicide prevention. There, that's it–I'm done. Take care. Good luck with your grief! I truly wish I could stop there, but that would defeat the purpose of helping others, which is what this journey is all about now. Helping others who are on this path and trying to help others avoid this route altogether. I can't leave you like this because this journey has not been easy, and I want to make yours easier. So, let's unpack the two very different reactions that I had to the losses of Mark (1983) and Matthew (1994).

I am one of five kids born to our parents. Mark was the second-oldest child; I was the middle child, and Matthew was the youngest child. When Mark died, I was a junior at West Virginia University, and I went home for the funeral on a

Thursday, and I was back on campus by Tuesday. In and out, no time for feelings, and when I got back to campus, I started drinking heavily. I was drinking already because the minimum age for alcohol back then was 18, and as a 20-year-old, I took full advantage of it. Looking back, this is a common occurrence for people dealing with a trauma: self-medication. In retrospect, I would seriously counsel against this. I had access to student services and counseling; I just didn't go. Went to a prayer group like twice and then blew it off. I had some positive places to go; I just chose not to use them. I now know what positive coping skills look like for me, and I know what negative coping skills look like for me. Drinking excessive amounts of alcohol—that's a negative coping skill, for sure. I truly thought I could self-medicate my pain away—WRONG! Everybody is recovering from something, and drugs and alcohol do not have a place in your recovery in any type of grief.

Now here's why alcohol and drugs should be pushed to the side as you recover from your loss:

While I was drinking at a high level (no pun intended), my brother Matthew was drinking while grieving at a whole other level. Eleven years after we lost Mark, we lost Matt. In a drunken stupor with access to lethal means, Matt was gone. Insert every curse word you know right here! I still cannot believe that after Mark died, we let Matthew slip past our fingers. It's just different when it's your younger brother. I should have been looking out for him, but I was too busy in my little bubble. I get that you must take care of yourself but keep your head on a swivel and try to look out for others that may be in a downward spiral. My head was not on right, so how could I possibly look out for others? I try not to beat myself up too badly about this loss (easier typed than done), but I now know that having lost someone to a suicide is a risk factor. I just wish I knew it back then. Reminder, these are my thoughts and feelings, and as I get older, I am often reminded that they could be wrong. I still have these feelings from time to time, and I have to remind myself to cut myself a break. I didn't do what my brothers did, and I may not have been able to stop any of this, but here we are. Here we f*cking are.

Life after Matthew was brutal because I did not numb the pain with anything. I got hammered the night of his funeral but did not touch a drop after that. I was too depressed, and alcohol is a depressant. I decided to take a time out, and I am happy to report that I am still sober after all these years. Yay me, but the lesson here is for you. Attack your loss with a sober mind, please! I cannot stress this point hard enough. I always thought that when I was better, I would go back to partying and drinking; you know, when I was happy again. But somewhere along the way, I fell in love with sobriety, and that's okay with me. I like not drinking alcohol, and so does everyone around me. At least that's what they tell me. Who knows what they say behind my back, but when they need a ride home from the bar, who's their buddy? ME!!!

There is a side story worth telling here, and it involves my faith (or lack thereof) after burying my second brother to suicide. I was sort of pissed at God, and who can blame me? I had just buried my second brother to suicide, and I was not a happy camper. On top of this loss, my then wife and I were having trouble conceiving. The doctors were working on her thyroid gland, and after they were done with her, they were going to turn their attention to me, and I did not want to go through that exam. So, one night in our guest bathroom I shook my fist at the sky and told God that I did not care what he wanted, I wanted a baby and now! If he granted me this wish, I would never drink again. A deal is a deal, and I got my son Martin, and God got me sober. I needed to be sober after this trauma, and I took it one step further and went and saw a counselor. I should have done this after losing my first brother! I highly recommend to any and all who will listen to me to go see a professional, especially after the loss of a loved one to suicide. So, if you are keeping score: professional counseling and sobriety is kicking the crap out of drinking and drugs when it comes to recovering! You're going to have to trust me on this one.

Michael

by Govan Martin

SUICIDE. Suicide in my family … *No way*. Suicide was something that happened to "other families." These were some of the thoughts that were going through my head in the aftermath of my brother's suicide.

I thought our family life was soooooo boring and "normal." There was just the four of us in our family: Mom, Dad, my brother Michael, and myself. We lived in Harrisburg, Pennsylvania. My dad was a Pennsylvania State Trooper, and my mom was a housewife. I was the older brother by only 11 months. Mom and Dad brought us up in a pretty strict household. Church and school were always the priorities while growing up. During half of my teen years, I thought of becoming a priest. More than anything, family always came first. I can remember my dad saying that we should *always* protect each other: "If one brother gets in a fight, then the other brother better be there to fight also." I want to say that, for the most part, it always seemed to be the case that I was always there for my brother in a fight. I wonder, though, what did I miss in his 16 years of his life?

Nothing ever seemed out of the ordinary those first 17 years of my life. Life was going pretty well for me. I had been a lifeguard since I was 15 years old, and I LOVED that job. Being out in the sun and especially the girls. That was the end of the priest vocation thoughts!

Then *change* happened. That perfect picture of "family" took a huge left turn when my parents separated in September 1979. How could they be getting a divorce when they didn't even fight? I could count on one hand the times I heard them fight. No one else that I knew, family or friends, had gone through their parents getting a divorce. Our family changed from that point on. I remember taking some anger out on Michael. He seemed to be on my dad's side, and I was on my mom's side. There would be arguments or punching battles, on and off, for a few months. About two months later, in November on a car ride back from running errands for my dad, Michael told me he wanted to kill himself, that there wasn't anything worth living for. I was in shock and didn't know what to say. I think I said something like, "Why would you want to do that?" Michael didn't say anything else and just stared out the car window the rest of the ride home. As soon as I got home, I told my dad. Dad immediately talked to Michael and told me about an hour later after he was done talking to Michael, that he would be okay. I never really thought about it after he told me.

In January 1980, I had my *first girlfriend.* I was excited for the positive new change in my life, especially after my mom and dad's separation. I was very shy and kept everything inside for pretty much all my life, but I saw that changing with my girlfriend.

January 30, 1980

Michael approached me in the middle of the school day and asked if he could borrow the car to go home because he forgot his homework. I didn't think anything about it and gave him the keys. Michael never came back, and I still didn't think that anything was wrong. I ended up walking home from school that day. I saw the car in front of our house and tried to get into the house through the front door. I rang the doorbell, and he didn't answer. The door was locked, so I had to go thought the basement to get in. As I entered the basement, I was yelling, "Michael! Michael, what are you doing?" I went upstairs and found Michael lying on the floor. I bolted out of the house and ran down the street to my friend's house. I remember pounding at the door and half collapsing on their porch. I don't remember who came out first, but my friend and his dad just started running towards my house. I followed them but slowed up because I didn't want to go back. I got to the doorway, and I felt this imaginary barrier keeping me out. I kept on hearing my friend's dad saying, "Michael, Michael." Before I knew it, a few ambulances arrived. About 15 minutes later, I saw my dad get out of an unmarked police car and go inside. I was just numb and in shock. I ended up back at my friend's house as my dad went to the hospital.

About an hour later my dad walked through the door and just looked at me. He didn't say a word as I looked at his face knowing what he was going to tell me … Michael had died. I just remembered sobbing and wailing, "This can't be happening." I remember wanting to rip out my eyes and not have that image implanted in my brain. My immediate thought went to … *This is all my fault ... How could I have let this happen*! Michael told me that he wanted to kill himself, and I didn't protect him. As I look back on this years later, I still find it hard to relinquish that guilt. That "guilt" was, and still is, the force that drives me into preventing suicide. I still struggle *every day* with the guilt, but I DO KNOW through therapy and forgiving myself that it was not my fault.

The next few days before the funeral were a blur. It seemed that I slept through most of those days trying to forget, hoping that I would wake up and it would all be some ugly dream. The most significant moment of those few days happened just minutes before the funeral started. I met the priest who was presiding over the funeral and made a quick confession so that I could take communion. After that was finished, I asked him the question that I had been dreading most of all: "Is Michael going to Hell?" He answered me by saying something like, "If your brother was in that much pain to take his own life, then God would not add to his pain. So no, I don't believe your brother is in Hell and that God is looking after him." It seemed that a heavy burden had been taken off me and brought me some kind of peace. I cannot thank that Priest enough. If he would have told me a different answer, I honestly don't know how that moment would have shaped my life.

After the funeral, the only person I wanted to see was my girlfriend. I went over to her house not knowing what she, or what her family, would say. I walked in the house, and she gave me a much-needed hug. I sat down in their living room and her dad, Mr. S, ordered everyone out of the room and said that he wanted to talk to me alone. After they left the room, Mr. S just looked at me and said, "Govan, I am so sorry for what happened. If there is anything that I can do for you, just let me know. I promise that our family will be here for you no matter what." I felt so comforted by what he said. Part of me thought he was just being nice, but I wanted so much to believe what he was telling me. Mr. S was really the *only* person who addressed what had happened and gave me permission to talk about it if I wanted to.

For the next nine months, I tried to ignore what happened to Michael. My total focus was spending time with my girlfriend. Her family treated me like I was a part of their family. My other friends acted like nothing happened. No one in school ever addressed it other than a few friends saying that they were sorry. I didn't really care about anything else other than my girlfriend and her family. I didn't care about school or college … *nothing*! That happiness was short-lived.

Nine months after Michael's death, I was blindsided when my girlfriend told me that she didn't want to see me anymore. I think that I held on so tight to that relationship that I smothered her. I was devastated because she and her family had literally become my lifeline. Then the proverbial crash happened. Everything that I was barely holding together just collapsed. I called it '*the trifecta*' (parents separating, Michael dying, and girlfriend breaking up with me), which made me fall apart in every which way. I was barely 18. I thought, "What else can happen to me?"

For the next few years, I was just numb. I didn't do well in school and didn't care. I remember crying a lot and feeling very alone. I still had my friends, but I didn't feel I could talk to them about any of it! There was a lot of blame and strong feelings from my family after Michael's death. The sad part of all that is that I blamed myself and no one else. All those strong feelings have lessened over time from my family, but as I said above, the struggle for blaming myself is always ongoing.

In 1983, three years after Michael died, I entered the Pennsylvania State Police Academy as I followed in my dad's footsteps and became a Trooper myself. I loved being a Trooper: great job, good money, and it gave me confidence in myself that I had never had before.

One *huge* pivotal moment came to me in 1984. I was still living at home with my dad. I had just gotten home from work and was watching TV in my bedroom. I was half asleep. All of a sudden, the door opened halfway, and it was Michael. He just looked in, stood there for a second, and slowly closed the door. I bolted out of my bed and ran down the hallway searching the house. He wasn't there, of course, and I didn't know what to think of it at the time. Over the years, I came to realize that for me, this was God's way of telling me that Michael was okay and that he, in a way, became my guardian angel taking care of me. Thank you, God, for that amazing gift!

In 1991, I started dating someone who I really liked and connected with. What I liked about 'J' was her honesty and her smile. In the first few weeks of dating, 'J' told me that she had attempted suicide when she was 18. She told me that she was still taking anti-depressants and still seeing a therapist from time to time. Things didn't work out after a few months, but we still stayed in touch. A few months later, I received a phone call from her friend telling me that 'J' had died by suicide. Her suicide just crushed me … not only for losing her but feeling like *I failed again*! I immediately went back to thoughts of Michael and the guilt I felt associated with his death. Her death immediately set me back emotionally and mentally … guilt, self-blame, shame, and responsibility for their deaths. More than anything, I felt that I had let them down and that I failed them in some way. The "my fault" feeling was just plastered in my brain during the next couple of years.

In 1998, I transferred into the Peer Support Program in the Pennsylvania State Police. This unit worked with other police officers who were experiencing personal, emotional, psychological, or related medical problems. Our main job was to listen, and if need be, refer the person to an appropriate mental health professional or other professional who would best be able to help that person, including those who were considering suicide. In all the years that I was in that unit, there was no greater reward than knowing that those who I did help that were considering suicide are still alive today! My Peer Support training showed me that *listening* and *caring* are the best ways to help others. This was another positive step into helping me heal. I also realized that peer support was a way to help and *save* others, because I couldn't save my own brother.

For the next several years, I found myself growing in confidence at work but failing at the relationships in my life. It seemed that I always ended up getting involved in relationships that were not good for me. The relationship that I thought could make a huge difference in my life turned out to be the one that made me totally fall apart. She lied, she cheated, and I still wanted her back. That relationship became so toxic and heartbreaking to the point of asking myself, and God, *why am I here, what purpose do I have in life*? It was the first time in my life I knew I needed to speak to someone professional.

I started to see Dr. N, who was a psychotherapist, in January 2000, and continued to talk with her over several years. Dr. N became a necessity for me after my relationship ended. Over the next few months, Dr. N talked about that relationship and other prior relationships. What really helped me is that she asked me about the other aspects of life, especially Michael. She let me talk about those losses and feelings of guilt about Michael and 'J'. After a few years, I finally had a breakthrough as to why I was feeling the way I did about myself. Dr. N asked me one day in a session to "look at the palm of your hands" and then to turn them over. She asked, "Do you see holes in your hands?" I said no, but after a few seconds it dawned on me exactly what she meant, and I started to cry. I realized at that moment that I was not responsible for saving my brother, 'J' or saving those relationships that were not good for me. I was not Christ (hence the holes in the hands) or responsible for saving everyone in the entire world because I couldn't save my brother. While my faith was a healing part of my life, my faith also hindered my healing process and exasperated my guilt. That was the epiphany and breakthrough that I needed. This was a huge healing factor and turning point in my life and one that I needed to hear.

I retired from the State Police in 2012 after 29 years and now am a Suicide Prevention Advocate. I am currently Chair of our Board of Directors for Prevent Suicide PA, the largest non-profit for suicide prevention in Pennsylvania. What has helped me over all these years was, and still is, helping other people.

There were several factors and important people in my life that helped me get to where I am now.

Mr. S (my ex-girlfriend's dad) made a promise from day one, and he kept it! I heard from Mr. S a few times every year after my relationship with his daughter ended. He would ask me how I was doing and made sure that I came over to his house at least a few times a year for dinner. He always asked, "Why don't you come over more often?" For over 30 years, until the day he died, he kept his promise to me: that I was part of their family and that I was always welcome in his house, and, more importantly, that he *cared*! He was an amazing man who continues to have a long-lasting impact on me.

Another person who had a major impact on me was a suicide prevention advocate, Ms. B. What a godsend she was! I met Ms. B at one of my first suicide advocacy committee meetings in 2007. Ms. B had mentioned in the meeting that she had also lost her brother to suicide. I waited to talk to her after the meeting just to say hello and to talk to her for a few minutes. Well, those few minutes turned into two hours outside in the parking lot. It was the *first* time I had talked to another survivor, and I didn't have to hide all those feelings on how I felt after my brother's suicide. It was like a huge weight had been lifted off me … someone else actually understood me! Ms. B was one of the leaders in the Suicide Prevention movement in Pennsylvania at that time and is now a leader nationally. She encouraged me to come to another meeting and get more involved in preventing suicide. Her passion and inspiration led me to the work that I do today. Thank you, Ms. B!

I have special friends in my life who have always been there for me. My best friends, who I fixed up in college, gave me the most wonderful gift that I have ever received when they asked me to be their kids' Godfather. Those three kids are truly my heart and soul!

The number one motivator, for me, that has always kept me going, is my faith. As I think back to Michael's funeral, I really believe that the priest cemented and enriched my faith even further by not judging my brother and expressing sorrow for what happened. I don't know how I would have felt if he told me that God had judged my brother. I do know that God is good and even after all the challenges in my life, I still have so much to be thankful for.

I know that working out for me is very important in my everyday life. I even ran a couple of marathons and lots of other races, which is, mentally and physically, great for me.

More importantly, what I have learned is that life is full of struggles, but there is *always* someone who cares, even when you feel alone. I have great friends and family, but sometimes that isn't enough. We have to seek out those other things that get us through the hardships of everyday life, most especially the loss of our sibling.

Here are a couple of things that I would recommend to sibling loss survivors.

1) *Don't be afraid to reach out to a mental health professional* (psychologist, psychiatrist, therapist, etc.). No matter what your age and gender, there is no shame in going to see a mental health professional. As the Nike slogan states, "Just Do It"!! Anyone and everyone can benefit from talking to someone who

knows how to help. If you don't like the person you are seeing, find someone else.

2) *Seek out survivor groups.* I wish that I would have talked to a fellow loss survivor when Michael died, and I didn't receive that essential gift until 27 years later. Survivors of loss can empathize with our thoughts and feelings and hopefully not judge.
3) *It is okay to feel—or even not to feel.* Don't think that you have to feel a certain way after the loss. You may have a multitude of emotions, or you may be just numb to what's going on. Feelings, or lack of them, *are* normal. Be good to yourself and allow yourself to just go through the loss of your sibling.
4) *Find your stress reliever.* You will have many people telling you that you have to do this or that; however, find whatever makes you feel good and gets you through the day. Run, work out, play video games, travel, journal, read a book, watch *Seinfeld,* etc. Find that Me-Time moment for yourself every day! It must be something that *you* like to do.
5) *Take things one minute, one hour, one day at a time.* You can get through this. Sometimes it is just putting one foot in front of the other; sometimes it's just making up your bed, and sometimes it's just allowing yourself to smile, but it can get better, even if it does seem like the pain will last forever. Don't forget: *You are not alone*!

The wonderful editor of this book asked me to think about what I would tell my younger self after Michael died. Such an insightful question and one that took me awhile to think about.

The number one thing that I would say to my younger self is, "It's going to be okay" (and give myself a big hug). I would say that it is going to take some time, that you will have ups and downs, and that you will never get over Michael, but you will heal. The second thing I would tell myself is to *forgive myself* and that it wasn't my fault (this is still difficult for me to realize today). I would also tell myself to *trust more* and not be afraid that those closest to me were going to leave or hurt me.

One last thing in closing that I want to share with other survivors of loss is: "*There is hope ... there is healing.*" However, healing does take time. Healing doesn't happen overnight or may not happen in months or years, but it does come, if you let it. I never will get over losing my Michael. *Never*. But I have healed. Do I still cry sometimes? Sure. Do I still feel guilty? Yes ... But I know that there is a peace that took me many years to build and happen. Healing came for me by helping others and letting others help me, and it can happen for you in however you choose to live your life. Surround yourself with positive people, other survivors if that helps. More importantly, surround yourself with people who love and care about *you*. To those reading this book: we are in a group that no one wants to belong to, but we can grieve together, we can heal together, and we can love and support one another. HOPE abounds!

Transforming Grief Over Time: The Long View

by Larry Berkowitz

Deep in the pain of the recent loss of his sibling, someone recently asked me how long this pain lasts. It was a good question, filled with the pressing need to know if the penetrating pain would remit. With the hindsight of over 40 years now since the day I returned home from high school to find that my sister, Helene, had died by suicide, here is an approximation of what I said: The pain is intense and is measured in minutes, hours, and days for the first months to year, with occasional periods of relief. After that, there are some respites from the intensity of the pain—much deep sadness and warmth from some memories, and lots of asking "why?" In those early years, thinking of my sister and trying to make sense of the loss occupied much of my consciousness. As time continued, there was always the feeling of a hole in my life, but not the searing pain of the early days. I once wondered when I would find "closure" to the pain and loss but have since come to dislike the notion of closure. Loss doesn't "wrap up"—rather, the meaning of our loss changes and evolves.

Early on, as a psychology major in college, I set out to research and understand suicide. For me, learning helped. However, the usual conundrums remained: how to answer when someone asks how many brothers or sisters I had. Early on, that question brought me up short. Often I'd say "one." Other times, "two." With the comfort of time, I am totally secure saying, "I grew up with two sisters, but one has been gone for quite some time now." There was the agonizing wondering if I could have done something to help, wondering if I had missed something that could have prevented the tragedy. Those questions abated with time, as I realized that I really could not have done anything different with the information I had at the time.

There were years where I really did not talk much about the suicide loss of my sister with anyone other than my surviving sister. I wish there had been survivor support groups when my sister died, as I would have appreciated having others to talk to who had a similar experience. However, I was thrilled when I found some people who had parallel losses and was drawn close to one of those people to whom I am now married. Our bond around losing a sibling was among the many things that brought us together. As the months and years progressed, the number of people whom I met who had significant losses surprised, saddened, and comforted me.

There are countless things I wish I had known. The intense anxiety I experienced starting around the first anniversary of my sister's death is not unusual for suicide loss survivors. The questioning about whether this would happen to me—again, fairly typical. The inability of my parents to talk about the loss—sadly typical for the time.

So what helped? Finding a few individuals with whom I could talk about the loss was number one. Meeting with therapists at different times in my journey to have a place to share and shape my understanding of the impact of the loss. Especially helpful has been a therapist who acknowledged that he lost a close friend to suicide in his past. As my career as a psychologist developed, I began to attend my state conference on suicide prevention, intervention, and postvention. At first, attending those conferences brought intense anxiety, but I was introduced to a community of people who publicly identified themselves as suicide loss survivors. Hearing them speak aloud about their losses awed and strengthened me.

When the 18-year-old daughter of a close friend died by suicide, I decided it was time to step off the sidelines and into the active work of suicide prevention. The program I now direct provides suicide postvention services to schools, communities, and workplaces. We conduct trainings on suicide prevention and management of suicide risk for mental health professionals and schoolteachers.

In my work and as an attendee at the annual conferences of the American Association of Suicidology (AAS), my state's suicide prevention conference, and occasional international conferences, I have found a way to honor the life and memory of my sister, to be in the community of others who have grieved and found ways to say good bye to the people they loved, and who have found that there are many ways that we can transform our grief into something constructive. There is amazing power in surrounding ourselves with others who have been on this journey and who have found ways to flourish. And it has been transformative to be a very small part of trying to solve the distressing problem of suicide and trying to bring comfort to those who are newly bereaved.

It has been a long journey, one that started by putting one foot in front of the other, a journey that required much patience early on and allowing others to provide support, comfort, and guidance along the way. I have no doubt that losing my sister to suicide changed the course of my life, but that has not been bad. I have met some amazing people and have witnessed impressive compassion and support by and between loss survivors. I learned at a young age that I have the strength to endure an incredibly difficult event—something I have reminded myself on countless occasions. The loss helped to put many things in perspective, and I truly learned to not "sweat the small stuff." The sadness and pain of the early days have been offset by a lifetime of wonderful events: the immense joy at the birth of children, watching them grow and thrive; deepening friendships and family connections that last over the years; a meaningful career with incredible colleagues. When I light a candle on the anniversary of my sister's death, I wonder what she would be like had she survived: would she have married? Have children? Been able to help when our parents were aging? But those are abstract, wistful thoughts now—mercifully without the pain from early days. I hope you find comfort in your journey and eventually in the embrace of warm memories.

IV

Closing Reflections

by Lena Heilmann

I am sitting down to write this brief conclusion in the first week of January 2019. The manuscript for *Still With Us: Voices of Sibling Suicide Loss Survivors* is almost complete, and another year is behind us. A new year ahead looms, filled with anniversaries, of moving through grief, of new memories, of remembering our pasts and pondering our futures without our siblings by our sides.

I want here to pause for a moment and offer a reflection on what it has meant for me to collect and edit these moving and inspiring essays written by survivors of sibling suicide loss.

When I set out to edit this collection, I envisioned the healing that this book would hopefully have on others who were grieving their loved ones lost to suicide. I imagined a book that would have helped me years ago, through my initial haze of early grief. I hoped that this book would also resonate with those further out in their grief and help readers move through healing, whatever these words mean to them.

What I did not foresee was how tremendously healing it would be for me to read submissions, to edit this collection, and to meet, through emails and phone calls and shared writing, the many brave and compassionate sibling survivors who participated in this project.

I began soliciting submissions in Fall 2017. I had just passed the five-year mark of my sister's death, and I realized that it was time to start this project that I had been thinking about for years. I was nervous to start something that might flare up my grief, and I was worried about the responsibility of others entrusting me with their stories.

I reminded myself of what I have learned in grief: Surviving my sister's death was, and is, the hardest thing I have ever done. Nothing else will be as hard as continuing to live after her death, so I know I have the strength to do the hard things.

When the essays started coming into my inbox a few months after I sent out the initial Call for Submissions, I was nervous, elated, and curious. As I began to read the first few submissions, I became overwhelmed by emotions. In my hands I held stories of strength and grief and post-traumatic growth from people all along a spectrum of grief journeys. Although I had made it through five years of grief, I could not imagine what a long-term future of my grief could look like. I was so grateful to be reading stories from other sibling survivors of suicide loss who showed me how one can continue to exist, to live a meaningful life with the capacity for joy, all while carrying our siblings' memory.

As the title of this collection states, our siblings are *still with us*.

Beyond my own healing that came from reading these amazing essays, I am honored and humbled that so many people entrusted me with their stories. If you have ever shared your own story publicly, you may know of the raw vulnerability that can come with translating your thoughts, your hopes and fears, your visible and invisible emotions into text, and sending them out into the world, where they exist on their own, on the written page. It can be absolutely terrifying.

And, compounding the vulnerability of sharing our stories is the responsibility of sharing the legacies of those we have loved and continue to love and whose deaths are devastating, traumatic, and confusing. Writing about our siblings is a great responsibility. We want to be honest to them, honest to ourselves, and honest to our readers. I am so grateful for being able to bring these essays together, in conversation with one another, to be shared with other survivors.

All of the authors in this collection have trusted me with honoring their siblings' memories and lives. I hope I have made them, and our siblings, proud with this collection.

Everything I do is in honor of my sister, Danielle. I love her with all my heart and will forever try to be the best big sister I can be.

Thank you to all the authors in this piece for sharing your journey with me and with those who are reading these words. I am so grateful.

With love,
Lena

Further Reading:

Books and Articles that Address Losing a Sibling to Suicide

Sara Swan Miller's collection of essays about surviving sibling suicide loss titled *An Empty Chair: Living in the Wake of a Sibling's Suicide* (2000) offers essays by sibling survivors that encompass a variety of feelings, repurcussions for family, friends, strangers, and relationships, and on sibling issues.

Michelle L. Rusk (formerly Linn-Gust) writes about her journey as a sibling survivor of suicide loss in *Do They Have Bad Days in Heaven? Surviving the Suicide Loss of a Sibling* (2001). Rusk talks about her sibling relationship with her sister Denise, who died by suicide in 1993, and offers a message of hope and survival.

T. J. Wray's *Surviving the Death of a Sibling: Living Through Grief When an Adult Sibling Dies* (2003) combines her own loss of her brother with her professional insight into the topic of adult sibling grief. The scope of Wray's book extends beyond suicide to include a broader understanding of adult sibling loss.

In *Seeking Hope: Stories of the Suicide Bereaved* (2011), edited by Michelle Rusk (formerly Linn-Gust) and Julie Cerel, survivors of sibling loss share stories of the impact of suicide on their lives. Some authors in the collection have lost siblings; some authors have lost other family or community members.

Nathan S. Wagner writes about losing his brother Brian to suicide in 2002 in *Sibling Suicide: Journey from Despair to Hope* (2016). Wagner's overarching premise is, "If I can do it, so can you" (p. XIX), and this solidarity with other sibling survivors of suicide loss offers an empathetic book to others who are surviving this traumatic loss.

Magdaline Halous DeSousa, who lost her brother John to suicide, discusses her personal grief journey and how sibling suicide loss survivors are often overlooked in her book *The Forgotten Mourners: Sibling Survivors of Suicide* (2012).

Comedic author David Sedaris writes about losing his sister Tiffany to suicide in 2013. In his piece "Now We Are Five" (October 28, 2013) in *The New Yorker*, Sedaris explores complex reactions to losing a sibling to suicide.

The anonymously written "What My Sister's Suicide Taught Me" (September 29, 2015) in *Verily* speaks to the author's pain of losing their sister, Lissa, to suicide and how the author's views on what is important in life and what is trivial have changed.

Samantha Seigler writes "A Letter to Someone Who Lost a Sibling to Suicide" (January, 2017) in *The Mighty*. She includes thoughts about how to answer the question, "How many siblings do you have?" and how a sibling's death may change family dynamics for surviving siblings.

In *The Mighty* article, "What It Means to be a 'Mid-Term' Survivor of Suicide Loss" (January 31, 2017), Lena Heilmann discusses her grief after losing her sister Danielle to suicide in 2012 and shares how she changed careers to address her grief and suicide prevention more fully and as a way to honor her sister.

In an NPR piece titled "After a Suicide, Sibling Survivors are Often Overlooked" (August 25, 2017), Cheryl Platzman Weinstock addresses the pain surviving siblings feel, as well current research on the topic of suicide loss and sibling loss.

Angela Skujin's article in *Vice*, "What It's Like to Lose a Sibling to Suicide" (March 13, 2018), includes anecdotes from surviving sibling loss survivors as well as professional insight into sibling grief, which society rarely acknowledges.

CNN's Anderson Cooper lost his brother Carter to suicide almost 30 years ago. In his article "Thirty years after my brother's death, I still ask why" (June 24, 2018), Cooper writes about living without knowing the "why" of a suicide death and the journey of being a sibling survivor of suicide loss.

Suicide Prevention Organizations and Lived Experience Resources

Suicide Prevention Organizations

American Foundation for Suicide Prevention (AFSP) – AFSP.org

American Association of Suicidology (AAS) – suicidology.org

International Association of Suicide Prevention (IASP) – iasp.info

National Action Alliance for Suicide Prevention – theactionalliance.org

National Suicide Prevention Lifeline – suicidepreventionlifeline.org

The Trans Lifeline – translifeline.org

The Trevor Project – trevorproject.org

Resources for Supporting Lived Experience

Live Through This – livethroughthis.org

The Mighty – themighty.com/topic/suicide-loss-survivors

Speaking of Suicide – speakingofsuicide.com

On Inclusivity and Next Steps

by Lena Heilmann

When I first set out to solicit essays for *Still With Us*, I thought deeply about people whose lived experiences are often not seen or heard in the fields of suicide prevention and suicide loss. I shared my intention to be inclusive and center diverse identities and experiences in the Call for Submissions. All of the essays I received are powerful and share a variety of experiences, and I am so grateful for every submission in this collection.

I would like to acknowledge that there are people and communities whose experiences and identities are underrepresented and/or non-existent in this book. As a person with multiple overlapping identities (some of which hold more historical power than others), I believe it is important to point this gap out for at least two major reasons: the first is that people from marginalized communities often face additional barriers and hurdles in their lives, which can include experiences of discrimination and/or historical trauma.

The second reason is to acknowledge that certain communities' loss narratives and experiences have been elevated above others. Lived experience stories from marginalized communities are often disproportionately impacted by this imbalance.

I will continue working on recognizing and addressing the gaps in whose stories are shared and centered. All of us who have identities that are more frequently centered can continue to work to make suicide loss and suicide prevention spaces more inclusive as well as build the trust of those who have lost someone to suicide who do not feel safe in sharing their stories publicly.

If you would like to talk to me about representation and inclusivity in this book, or if you might be interested in sharing your experience as a sibling suicide loss survivor for a future edition, volume, or iteration of this project, please email me at *lenasurvivingsiblingsuicide@gmail.com*.

About the Authors

Amy Thrasher

Amy Thrasher lives in a canyon in Colorado with her husband and their hound dog. She is a speech-language pathologist serving children with communication needs and their families. She enjoys dabbling in different art media, from embroidery to welding, and could be considered a hack of all trades. While profoundly affected by the loss of her older sister to suicide, she continues to find her way.

Barbara Kulka

I am Barbara Kulka. I'm a sister, a wife, a daughter, a mother and an awesome grandmother. I love to make quilts, travel, and read. I'm retired after a career in information management. I've volunteered my whole life and enjoy seeing people happy!

Corbin J. Standley

Corbin J. Standley lost his older brother, David, to suicide in June of 2010. Since that time, he has worked with numerous organizations to bring about awareness for suicide prevention in Utah and Michigan. He has served as a board member for the Utah Chapter of the American Foundation for Suicide Prevention (AFSP), a member of the NUHOPE Task Force, and a board member for the Legacy Survivors Group. He is currently a member of the Tri-County Lifesavers Coalition in mid-Michigan and serves on the Board of Directors for the Michigan Chapter of AFSP.

Corbin has served as a keynote speaker, featured speaker, panelist, and moderator throughout Utah and Michigan. These events have covered topics such as academic success and resume building, community mental health, student mental health, suicide prevention, and coping with grief. He holds a Bachelor of Science degree in Psychology from Weber State University. Currently, he is a doctoral student and University Distinguished Fellow in the Ecological-Community Psychology Program at Michigan State University. His current research explores the demographic variables that contribute to suicide risk among youth and how those variables intersect with one another, as well as the socioecological factors that protect against suicidality with a particular focus on the role of social support.

Dennis Gillan

Dennis lost two brothers to suicide, and after years of grieving and healing, he now shares his story with anyone who will listen! A gifted speaker and storyteller, Dennis uses the losses of his brothers, Mark and Matthew, to raise awareness about mental health and suicide prevention. Dennis lives in Greenville, SC so he can be close to his two adult sons. You can reach Dennis by visiting www.dennisgillan.com

Elliat Graney-Saucke

Elliat Graney-Saucke is a 35-year-old documentary filmmaker and cultural organizer based in the Pacific Northwest. She is grateful to have had the opportunity to share a glimpse of the experience of losing her sister and looks forward to someday expanding upon this story and the pain and beautify of her sister's life. You are not alone … we are not alone. Thank you for reading, and for taking care of yourself by reading this book. And thank you, Lena, for making it.

Emily Reitenbach-Molina

Emily Reitenbach-Molina lost her only and older sister Shannon at the age of 36 to suicide on 7/8/10 after Shannon battled half her life with an eating disorder. Emily was only 34 at the time of her sister's death. Since the passing of her sister, Emily has tried to turn her pain into purpose by becoming a local advocate for the American Foundation for Suicide Prevention (AFSP). She has attended local and national advocacy days to speak about the importance of mental health and funding suicide prevention work. Emily works for a local high school and feels that the courses she's taken in Applied Suicide Intervention Skills Training (ASIST) and Youth Mental Health First Aid (YMHFA) have provided the skills needed to help with teenagers who suffer in silence.

On a more personal level, Emily, along with her parents and husband, have raised awareness and funds for three local NPOs in Cincinnati: AFSP, Mental Health America, and National Eating Disorder Association by selling "Shannon's Butterflies" shirts. Every year they designate a day to "Spread Your Wings For Awareness" and ask anyone with a Shannon's Butterflies shirt to wear it and to help begin life-saving conversations that so many shy away from. The feedback has been amazing! There are butterflies all over the country and even one in Europe.

Emily has spoken at public events and vigils around Cincinnati and Northern Kentucky about how one survives a suicide loss and how we each can play a part in saving lives. Emily takes her sister's bear that Shannon named "HOPE" to all the events. It's a reminder to herself that, with hope, all things are possible. Emily will continue to be the voice for Shannon and all the other souls we have loved and lost too soon.

Govan Martin

Govan A. Martin III is currently the Chair of Prevent Suicide PA, a non-profit organization in Pennsylvania. He is a survivor of his brother Michael who died by suicide in 1980. Govan served with the Pennsylvania State Police (PSP) from 1983 to 2012. After being a state policeman for 29 years, Govan became a full-time advocate for suicide prevention. Besides working with Prevent Suicide PA, Govan also conducts trainings around the country concerning suicide prevention and critical incident stress management.

Heather Sutherland

Heather Sutherland lives in the UK. She has been and done a lot of different things and has lived in a lot of places (including Mexico); she aims to live life to the fullest she possibly can! She lost her brother, Martin, to suicide in 2011 when she was 30 years old, and this changed so much about her and her perspectives on life. It has not been easy for her to learn to live with the loss of her brother (some days she is still learning), but she remains passionate about helping others where she can, most importantly talking and writing about mental ill health and suicide loss as a means to lessening stigma. (Other writing can be seen on Heather's blog: https://hermanamam.wordpress.com/)

Helio Nowell

33, married and father. Surviving with my parents and siblings.

Jen

I am the youngest of three siblings. My brother was 12 years older than me, and we grew closer as we aged. My hobbies include photography, camping, hiking, and spending time with my kids and dog. What gives me hope? While taking pictures of people and talking openly about my brother's passing, I have heard other people's stories. Some people have cried and told me that I was the first person they have told the real reason that a loved one passed. I reassure them: there is no shame in suicide loss. And talking about it may give others the strength to reach out for help.

Larry Berkowitz

Larry Berkowitz is the Director and co-founder of Riverside Trauma Center in Needham, Massachusetts and holds an appointment as a Teaching Associate in Psychology, Part Time, at Harvard Medical School. He is a member of the Executive Committee of the Massachusetts Coalition for Suicide Prevention, and was a member of the Survivors of Suicide Loss Task Force of the National Action Alliance for Suicide Prevention. A licensed Psychologist in Massachusetts, he specializes in working with children, adolescents and families. He trains extensively on suicide prevention, assessment and management of suicide, and postvention activities to contain suicide contagion in schools and communities. Dr. Berkowitz has consulted with numerous schools, organizations and communities on responding to traumatic events and clinical issues for the past 25 years, and leads a state-wide behavioral health trauma response network. He has been married for over 35 years and has two amazing, thoughtful, and talented adult daughters.

Lena Heilmann

Lena lost her sister Danielle to suicide in 2012. In response to this traumatic loss and as a way to honor her sister, Lena left academia and her career as a college professor to work full-time in suicide prevention. Now, Lena merges her lived experience and lived expertise with her professional work, driven by a mission to create empathy, connect survivors, share stories, and find community. Lena's grief and loss survivor identity remain centered in all that she does to help make this a world worth living in, because no one should have to live in suicidal despair.

Lynne

Lynne, 36 years old. Married and mother of twins, preschool teacher. Ontario, Canada. I lost my younger brother in April 2012. I didn't go to therapy until about a year after. Luckily we have the Toronto Distress Center, where they provide suicide grief counselling for free. From that point on, I was able to move a bit forward towards coping and healing.

I especially owe my sanity to my fellow siblings on a social media group, who bring light when darkness takes over and everything else falls apart.

My days are full of children's laughter and tears. And from every bit of smile I see, I find hope. That the tears will come by less, and that I will be able to smile more.

Mary Costello

My name is Mary Costello. I am a single parent residing in New York, and I lost my brother and cousin to suicide in 2014. I struggle with my own mental health issue daily, but strive to find a balance that allows me to truly enjoy life. I find my balance in writing, adventures with my daughter, long drives, loud music, and beautiful views.

Michelle L. Rusk

Michelle L. Rusk, Ph.D., previously known as Michelle Linn-Gust, has inspired people worldwide for over twenty years to lead meaningful and authentic lives. She is a past president of the American Association of Suicidology and the author of ten books (three of them fiction novels), most recently, *Flowers by Day: Stars by Night: Finding Happiness after Loss and Change*. Moving beyond the many losses in her life—including the suicide of her younger sister and the deaths of her parents—today she focuses on inspiring others through living creatively with her lifestyle brand, Chelle Summer. Learn more about Michelle at www.chellesummer.com.

Sarah

Sarah loves dancing in the rain, birds, wind chimes, and long trail runs. She is a documentary filmmaker; telling stories that inspire healing and positive change. She loves to travel the world. Singing and songwriting are two of her greatest passions. She loves honeybees, star gazing, moon watching, sunshine, herbs, yoga, gardens, mangos, coconuts, and her three-year-old puppy Leikahh. She calls Colorado home, but loves the ocean too. Her ideal climate is tropical rainforest. She ran cross country for eight years. She enjoys having friends from all walks of life. She loves her family. She is 28 years old.

Shelby Drager

My name is Shelby Drager, I am 29 years old, and I have lived in Colorado since I was 2 years old. I have a fiancé, two surviving sisters, and my parents. I also have two sweet pups, Jewels and Piper! I love the outdoors: snowboarding, hiking, and traveling, as well as reading, writing, and singing. One of my biggest passions is animals, and I currently own a pet-sitting business.

Sally Spencer-Thomas

As a clinical psychologist, inspirational international speaker, impact entrepreneur, and survivor of suicide loss, Dr. Spencer-Thomas sees the issues of suicide prevention and mental health promotion from many perspectives. Dr. Spencer-Thomas was moved to work in suicide prevention after her younger brother, a Denver entrepreneur, died of suicide after a difficult battle with bipolar condition. Known nationally and internationally as an innovator in social change, Spencer-Thomas has helped start up multiple large-scale, gap filling efforts in mental health including the award-winning campaign "Man Therapy" (a program using humor to engage men in mental health) and the nation's first comprehensive workplace program designed to help employers with the successful prevention, intervention, and crisis management of suicide. A 2016 invited speaker at the White House, Spencer-Thomas' goal is to elevate the conversation and make suicide prevention a health and safety priority in our schools, workplaces, and communities.

In 2017 she delivered a TEDx Talk called "Stopping Suicide with Story" based in large part on her work as the founding board President for United Suicide Survivors International, a nonprofit dedicated to helping suicide loss and attempt survivors leverage their stories of living through despair into hope for cultural change (www.UniteSurvivors.org).

Spencer-Thomas has also held leadership positions for the National Action Alliance for Suicide Prevention, the International Association for Suicide Prevention, the American Association for Suicidology, and the National Suicide Prevention Lifeline.

She has a Doctorate in Clinical Psychology from the University of Denver, Masters in Non-profit Management from Regis University, a Bachelors in Psychology and Studio Art with a Minor in Economics from Bowdoin College. She has written four books on mental health and violence prevention. She lives with her partner and three sons in Conifer, Colorado.

Connect with Dr. Spencer-Thomas by visiting her website and signing up for her newsletter at www.SallySpencerThomas.com and by following her on Facebook @DrSallySpeaks, Twitter @

sspencerthomas and LinkedIn. Come "elevate the conversation" with her by participating in her monthly podcasts, blogs and twitter chats!

Tana Nash

After the suicides of her grandmother in 1987 and her only sister and sibling in December 2006, Tana combined her professional skills in sales, marketing, and communications from twenty years as an advertising sales representative with her passion for suicide prevention advocacy and was the Executive Director for both the Waterloo Region Suicide Prevention Council and the Canadian Association for Suicide Prevention. Education, awareness, engaging stakeholders to provide increased and better services, and action were the key focuses. Tana was instrumental in having Bill C-300, a federal framework for suicide prevention in Canada, tabled in the House of Commons. This bill became law in December of 2012. Although Tana continues to advocate for suicide prevention, she has taken a step back from such a public role to spend time with her husband and sister's child.

Vanessa McGann

Vanessa McGann, Ph.D., is a clinical psychologist with a private practice specializing in traumatic loss in New York City. She is the Director of Extern Training and a counselor at the New School as well as a faculty member of the Child Psychotherapy Program of the William Alanson White Institute. She chairs the Loss Division and is co-chair of the Clinician-Survivor Task Force for the American Association for Suicidology. In addition, she consults on topics related to suicide and postvention to various schools, colleges, and agencies including the NY State Office of Mental Health. She also helped to create the guidelines of the Survivors of Suicide Task Force for the National Action Alliance for Suicide Prevention. She lost her sister to suicide in 2004.

WyKisha McKinney

WyKisha McKinney's fight against suicide began with the loss of her brother Johnny Madison, who died by suicide in 2004. Overwhelmed by grief after the death of her brother, WyKisha slipped into major depression which almost ended with her own suicide attempt. With the support of her husband and son, and the help of local organizations, she was able to get the help she needed to cope with her loss and manage her depression. As she journeyed through her healing process, she found solace in helping others. WyKisha can often be found sharing her story with different groups in the community, flying across the country to talk with legislators in our nation's capital, training crisis hotline volunteers, or coordinating the annual Out of the Darkness Community Walk.

When asked about her commitment to saving lives, WyKisha states, "Having experienced that kind of pain myself, I can't be at peace knowing that others are hurting like that. More and more people are silently struggling with depression and other mental illnesses and more families are losing their loved ones to suicide. Until they are strong enough to speak for themselves, I will do it for them. It's just my nature, I guess."

References:

Anonymous. (2015, September 29). What my sister's suicide taught me. Retrieved from *verilymag.com/2015/09/suicide-depression-mental-illness-losing-a-sibling-death-family-sisters-bipolar*

Cooper, A. (2018, June 24). Anderson Cooper: Thirty years after my brother's death, I still ask why. Retrieved from *cnn.com/2018/06/24/us/anderson-cooper-brother-suicide/index.html*

Halous DeSousa, M. (2012). *The forgotten mourners: Sibling survivors of suicide*. Outskirts Press.

Heilmann, L. (2017, January 31). What it's like to be a 'mid- term' survivor of suicide loss. Retrieved from *themighty.com/2017/01/mid-term-survivor-suicide-loss*

Linn-Gust, M. (2001). *Do they have bad days in Heaven? Surviving the suicide loss of a sibling*. Roswell, GA: Balton Press Atlanta.

Linn-Gust, M., & Cerel, J. (2011). *Seeking hope: Stories of the suicide bereaved.* Albuquerque, NM: Chellehead Works.

Miller, S. S. (2000). *An empty chair: Living in the wake of a sibling's suicide*. San Jose, CA: Writers Club Press.

Sedaris, D. (2013, October 28). Now we are five. Retrieved from *newyorker.com/magazine/2013/10/28/now-we-are-five*

Seigler, S. (2017, January 15). A letter for someone who lost a sibling to suicide. Retrieved from *themighty.com/2017/01/sibling-suicide-how-to-grieve*

Skujins, A. (2018, March 13). What it's like to lose a sibling to suicide. Retrieved from *vice.com/en_us/article/8xdzg4/what-its-like-to-lose-a-sibling-to-suicide*

Wagner, N. S. (2016). *Sibling suicide: Journey from despair to hope*. CreateSpace.

Weinstock, C. P., & NPR. (2017, August 25). After a suicide, sibling survivors are often overlooked. Retrieved from *kpbs.org/news/2017/aug/25/after-a-suicide-sibling-survivors-are-often*

Wray, T. J. (2003). *Surviving the death of a sibling: Living through grief when an adult brother or sister dies*. New York, NY: Three Rivers Press.

CPSIA information can be obtained
at www.ICGtesting.com
Printed in the USA
LVHW082350061021
699781LV00017B/141